BRIGHT NOTES

JUDE THE OBSCURE BY THOMAS HARDY

Intelligent Education

Nashville, Tennessee

BRIGHT NOTES: Jude the Obscure
www.BrightNotes.com

No part of this publication may be used or reproduced in any manner whatsoever without written permission, except in the case of brief quotations in critical articles and reviews. For permissions, contact Influence Publishers http://www.influencepublishers.com.

ISBN: 978-1-645424-86-4 (Paperback)
ISBN: 978-1-645424-87-1 (eBook)

Published in accordance with the U.S. Copyright Office Orphan Works and Mass Digitization report of the register of copyrights, June 2015.

Originally published by Monarch Press.
Ralph A. Ranald, 1965
2019 Edition published by Influence Publishers.

Interior design by Lapiz Digital Services. Cover Design by Thinkpen Designs.

Printed in the United States of America.

Library of Congress Cataloging-in-Publication Data forthcoming.
Names: Intelligent Education
Title: BRIGHT NOTES: Jude the Obscure
Subject: STU004000 STUDY AIDS / Book Notes

CONTENTS

1)	Introduction to Thomas Hardy	1
2)	Introduction to Jude the Obscure	7
3)	Textual Analysis	
	Part First	13
	Part Second	41
	Part Third	61
	Part Fourth	84
	Part Fifth	102
	Part Sixth	125
4)	Character Analyses	146
5)	Critical Commentary	154
6)	Essay Questions and Answers	159
7)	Bibliography	167

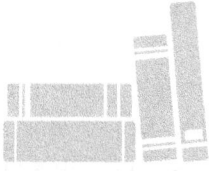

INTRODUCTION TO THOMAS HARDY

LIFE OF HARDY

Thomas Hardy, the son of a building contractor, was born in 1840 in a small town in Dorset, in southwestern England. He attended church regularly with his family, and later taught in the local Sunday school. As a boy he memorized all the services, and this knowledge underlies the frequent references to religion in his works. In addition, Thomas' father was a musician who played at church services, and the boy followed in his father's footsteps by learning to play the violin. This was the start of a lifelong interest in music, which also figures prominently in his books. Although young Hardy's education was not particularly good, there were books in his home and he read all he could. At the age of sixteen, he left school and was apprenticed to an architect. Hardy is thus one of the relatively few well-known English writers who did not have a university education (Shakespeare and Dickens are others). Although his formal studies stopped, he continued to educate himself. He would arise early in the morning and study for an hour or two before leaving for work. In this way he continued to read various Latin and English authors and also taught himself Greek. In 1862 he left the architect's office, well trained as a draftsman and with a considerable amount of reading behind him. At the age of twenty-two he left Dorset for London. There young Hardy came into contact for the first time with the advances of the modern world. It must be understood that life in the Dorset of the 1840s and 1850s had hardly changed in its broad outlines since the Middle Ages. It was nearly completely rural in character, and at that time was still, sufficiently isolated from the rest of the world for few of the industrial and mechanical aspects of modem civilization to have come to it. (Dorset provides the setting for most of Hardy's novels and stories, including those that are generally thought to be his best. Hardy, however, changed the name of Dorset to "Wessex," and he changed the names of all the towns he wrote of as well. A map of the Wessex country, with both the real and fictional names of the places that occur in Hardy's work, is to be found in the edition of *Tess of the d'Urbervilles* edited by Carl J. Weber—see Bibliography.) In London he worked as an architect. He also studied French, visited art galleries and the great London exposition, and continued his course of reading. During these years he wrote the first of his poems to survive. It is clear that he greatly expanded his mental horizons, but he paid a price for his excessive exertions—his health suffered and he was generally unhappy. In 1867 he returned to Dorset, but not as a full-time architect. He temporarily stopped writing poetry and made his first attempt at prose fiction. Hardy had reached a real crossroads in his life. By 1868 he had completed his first novel—*The Poor Man and the Lady*—which, though it was rejected, convinced him that he should continue his efforts at novel-writing. In the same year he did his last work as an architect, and it was during this time that he met the girl he was to marry. It was altogether a most crucial year for Hardy.

HIS NOVELS

All Hardy's novels were written during the next twenty-eight years. *The Poor Man and the Lady* was a slashing social satire, and when it was rejected Hardy switched to writing romances, stories with complicated plots and much sensational action. He began with *Desperate Remedies* in 1871, *Under the Greenwood Tree* (1872) and *A Pair of Blue Eyes* (1873). These books are highly autobiographical (as are the first novels of most writers), and they were reasonably well reviewed. *Under the Greenwood Tree* was the first of the novels to have a rural setting. Before, *A Pair of Blue Eyes* appeared as a book, it came out as a serial in a magazine, and this set a pattern—nearly all the rest of Hardy's novels were first published in this form. (This was a common practice for novelists in general in the nineteenth century.) In 1874 he published *Far from the Madding Crowd,* the earliest of the novels which are generally read today. This book received very favorable reviews, and Hardy followed it with *The Hand Ethelberta* in 1876. The latter work is not a pastoral novel because Hardy decided that he did not want to be identified in the public mind as a writer who could only write about "cows and sheep." Throughout his novel-writing career Hardy was very sensitive to the reading public, and he often acknowledged that he sought popularity. The next book Hardy composed is certainly among his best and most popular—*The Return of the Native* (1878). This was followed by several volumes which are not among his most successful efforts: *The Trumpet-Major* (1880), *A Loadicean* A1881), and *Two on a Tower* (1882). By this time Hardy was recognized to be one of England's leading novelists, and this reputation was greatly enhanced by the books that appeared in the next decade. This period of Hardy's career saw the production of those novels that have ensured him lasting fame. In 1886 there was *The Mayor of Casterbridge,* in 1887 *The Woodlanders;* 1891 saw *Tess of the d'Urbervilles,* and *Jude the Obscure,* the last novel he wrote, appeared in 1896. (*The Well-Beloved* came out in 1897, but it had been written in 1892.) Throughout these years Hardy was composing short stories as well as novels, and several volumes of these stories appeared, as follows: *Wessex Tales* (1888), *A Group of Noble Dames* (1891), and *Life's Little Ironies* (1894). (A last book of stories, *A Changed Man, The Waiting Supper, and Other Tales,* came out much later, in 1913.) After *Jude the Obscure* Hardy mainly wrote poetry. It should be remembered that he started out as a poet and had been composing poetry throughout the time he was writing novels. The last novels he published were all very controversial, and they caused Hardy to undergo some very severe criticism. This criticism, which sometimes amounted to personal abuse, combined with his continuing love for poetry and his newly won financial security, caused him to abandon the novel and return to poetry. *Wessex Poems*, which contained some of his earliest work, came out in 1898 and was received very well. In 1901 he published *Poems of the Past and Present.* The first part of his great epic poem *The Dynasts* appeared in 1903. It deals with the Napoleonic Wars and is one of the longest poems in English. The second and third parts came out in 1906 and 1908. The satirical title of *Time's Laughing-Stocks* (1909) indicates something of the bitter tone of this collection of ballad-like poems about sexual infidelity and unsuccessful marriage. It is thought that Hardy's own marriage was not especially happy, but its tensions were not to last much longer. In 1912 his wife Emma died. Hardy expressed his deep feeling for her in several of the poems that made up his next collection of verse: *Satires of Circumstance, Lyrics and Reveries* (1914). Hardy was then seventy-two, and the loss of his wife was a great shock. His life seemed to disintegrate, and he passed through two disastrous, disorganized years. In 1914, however, he married again, and his life once more regained its balance. In the same year the First World War broke out, but it did not check his inspiration. He continued to write, and in 1917 brought out *Moments of Vision and Miscellaneous Verses.* He followed this by *Late Lyrics and Earlier* (1922), the verse drama *The Queen of Cornwall* (1923), *Human Shows* (1925), and finally *Winter Words,* published posthumously in the year of his death, 1928.

HARDY'S TIME

The age in which Hardy wrote, sometimes called the late Victorian period (after Queen Victoria, who reigned from 1837 to 1901), was one of great change and many difficulties. In fact, in the Victorian period we can see the beginnings of many of the problems of our own time. English society was experiencing severe strains in its attempts to adjust to vast alterations in its structure, and *Tess of the d'Urbervilles* reflects its author's concern with several of the most pressing problems of his time. Hardy depicts the effects of the pressure of the new, urban, and industrial civilization on the old, rural, and agricultural life of Wessex. He exposes the hypocrisy of the rules that govern sexual behavior and the position of women in society. The third leading theme of the book is the question, especially acute in his day, of how to live in a time when religion no longer provided acceptable rules of conduct. Both Angel and Alec are typical young men of the age, sufficiently enlightened to reject the traditional standards, but unable to create new ones for themselves. Thus both are alone in relation to their society. *Tess* is one of the first novels to examine this theme (a major one ever since) of the effects of spiritual and moral isolation in modem society. Of course *Tess* is a novel and not a textbook on morals, and therefore these problems are not taken up in a systematic way; rather, they form the background of ideas and feelings against which the characters move and act.

THE NOVEL'S STRUCTURE

The structure of the novel has often been discussed. Thomas Hardy was an architect by training, and it is tempting to suppose that this background may have caused him to plan his novels as carefully as we know he did. Before he began to write, he worked out a detailed outline, including a table of important dates in the lives of his characters (for such a table on *Tess,* see the appendix of Weber's *Hardy of Wessex*). In the past Hardy's structural craftsmanship has often been praised, but today opinion has changed. Present-day critics still believe that a novel requires careful planning and construction, but they now think that the reader should not be aware of the craftsman at work. In Hardy, the reader is all too often conscious of the details of the structure (it is as if one were aware of all the carpentry in a house). Take, for instance, the rather mechanical alternation between spring and fall, and the fact that Tess is arrested at Stonehenge on June 1, just five years to the day that she set out to visit Trantridge. Nevertheless, if we do sometimes see the puppeteer a little too clearly behind the stage, there is no denying the cumulative power and effect of the tragedy that befalls Tess, and this is in large measure due to the careful plan of the book, obvious or not.

INTRODUCTION TO JUDE THE OBSCURE

BRIEF SUMMARY AND ANALYSIS

The novel is set by Hardy in and about the town of Christminster (actually Oxford) in the Wessex country, at a time roughly contemporary with its writing, that is, in the last two decades of the nineteenth century. Only two of the six parts of the novel are actually set in Christminster, but they are the two most important parts. Besides this, Christminster and its university are present in the consciousness of the central character from the first moment of the work to the last; thus it is the center about which all the action revolves.

The story deals with a young man, Jude Fawley, a stonemason by trade, an orphan by upbringing, who is consumed by the passion to rise above his birth and to become both a scholar and a famous and influential churchman, perhaps a bishop. He is intelligent and quick, and after being fired with the zeal for the learning which was most prized in the England of that historical period, that is classical learning and the ability to move easily in the Latin and Greek classics, Jude begins to study on his own while living with his aunt in the humble village of Marygreen where the first part of the novel is set. It is his village schoolmaster, Richard Phillotson, who inspires him with this design: just as Phillotson plans to leave his position and go to the university to win fame and a degree, so Jude determines that at his first opportunity he, too, will do exactly this.

For years, Jude helps his Aunt Drusilla in her small bakery, while he reads Latin and Greek, and develops into a passable but not an outstanding student. Hardy gives him credit for great achievement even to have gone this far, because he is working without a teacher. Technically, anyone having the qualifications could take and pass the entrance examinations for Oxford or Cambridge, and in the Middle Ages a number of scholarships and appointments (called "sizarships") had been reserved for boys like Jude: poor but intelligent and likely to become ornaments to the nation. But it may be that to win admission for a boy in Jude's circumstances, living in such an isolated rural area, is at this time impossible, unless he were an outstanding genius. And Hardy makes it clear that Jude is not this.

About his nineteenth birthday, Jude meets up with a coarse and rather sensual young woman, whose occupation, rather appropriately, is the tending of her father's pigs. All his life Jude is to have somewhat of a weakness - though not a really pronounced or excessive one, though it will damage him irrevocably-for liquor and for women. Arabella Donn, the name of the girl whom he meets by accident near her father's pigsty, decides that she wants to marry Jude, and by all means possible she works on this project until she has succeeded in entrapping him through his own good nature (see Character Analysis section for a detailed picture of Jude's strengths and weaknesses).

Jude and Arabella are married, but Jude quickly learns that this has been a horrible mistake on his part; Arabella had married him in order to escape from her unsatisfactory situation in her father's house and also out of physical desire, nothing more. Their marriage soon breaks up, and Jude, at the end of the first part, proceeds to Christminster. He has been a journeyman stonecutter, and proposes to earn his living by repairing churches and other stoneworks in Christminster while reading with a view to college entrance.

But he is side-tracked by the difficulty of doing the two jobs well. Besides this, he meets another young woman, Susanna Florence Mary Bridehead, who is his cousin and is an extreme contrast to Arabella. She is all intellect and etherealized emotion, with little of the physical about her - but Hardy implies that in her way she is just as much a creature of excess as is Arabella, and perhaps less honest. Certainly she is more destructive toward Jude. She has been working in an ecclesiastical-goods establishment, but she is not satisfied with this. Through the schoolmaster Richard Phillotson, whom she meets through Jude- Phillotson still teaching and having long ago given up his plan of gaining a degree - she becomes an apprentice teacher and a student at a teacher training college. She and Jude cannot marry: they are cousins, and Jude is still legally married to Arabella. In addition, Jude had been warned repeatedly by his Aunt Drusilla that there was something in the Fawley family line and blood which made their marriages inevitably unhappy, and that in view of this fatal curse it would be folly for Sue and Jude to marry.

Jude is rudely refused consideration for entrance into any of the colleges at Christminster. Meanwhile, he tells Sue of his prior marriage to Arabella. Hurt, and on the rebound, she becomes engaged to Phillotson, and is married to him, with Jude actually giving her away at the church. Jude takes to drink, mildly, and returns to his home, rather in disgrace, all of his glittering plans fallen to pieces.

But Sue's marriage to the much older Phillotson is very unhappy. They are obviously physically incompatible. Sue and Jude see more of each other, until finally they run away together. Meanwhile Arabella, who had gone to Australia with her parents, had returned. She had married bigamously a second time in Australia. She begs Jude not to give her secret away. In turn, she has another secret, but she will not at this time reveal it to Jude.

At Shaston, Jude and Sue meet again-Sue is living there with Phillotson. But suddenly she asks her husband for her freedom. She cannot stand living with him. Reluctantly he grants this request, although by doing so he ruins himself professionally and is forced to resign his teaching position. But Sue and Jude go off together, living at first as comrades. Neither can legally marry again. But they institute divorce proceedings respectively against Phillotson and Arabella, and are ultimately free to marry. Sue has been a questioner of society and its mores, while Jude is more conservative, but from this point on, the opinions of the two gradually become reversed, until at the end of the work, Jude is a complete skeptic while Sue is fanatically orthodox.

Though they are free to marry, they neglect to do so, for reasons which are rather obscure and lie in the character of Sue. Arabella precipitates their catastrophic downfall, for one day she appears; she and her "husband", the tavern-keeper Cartlett, having returned to England. She claims that she has a child by Jude, conceived right at the end of their marriage unknown even to her, and born over eight months after her arrival in Australia. Jude is not sure that the child is his, but he and Sue accept it and take care of the boy, a morose, withdrawn, and perfectly fantastic figure with the name of Little Father Time.

In the succeeding years, Jude and Sue have two children of their own. Jude's health fails from the heavy exertions of his trade. Again they are in Christminster. In a grand debacle, Little Father Time murders the two younger children of Sue and Jude and then kills himself, leaving the note: "Done because we are too menny." He is allegorically the embodiment of "the coming universal wish not to live." Sue is torn by feelings that she alone is guilty and that the deaths are punishments for her sins. She asks Phillotson to marry her again so that she can be subject to him; all she wants now is to be punished. And she advises Jude to remarry Arabella, whose second husband has now died.

As the novel concludes, Jude is married again to Arabella. He dies in Christminster on the anniversary of the deaths of his children, on Remembrance Day, a celebration of the university. Meanwhile, Sue continues to be married to Phillotson, though she has loved Jude to the end, but the marriage is a loveless one, and has been entered into by Sue, Hardy implies, out of a religious fanaticism and a wish for punishment.

The tale, with its dual marriages and reversals, is a strange one but does not seem unusual to our age in terms of the moral questions involved. But when the novel was published it evoked the most bitter reaction on the parts of some of Hardy's respectable contemporaries. A bishop ordered the text publicly burned, which increased its notoriety. It seemed to be an attack on the sanctity of marriage and the authority of the Church. But Hardy, in his Preface written in August, 1895, defended himself, saying: "For a novel addressed by a man to men and women of full age, which attempts to deal unaffectedly with the fret and fever, derision and disaster, that may press in the wake of the strongest passion known to humanity, and to point, without a mincing of words, the tragedy of unfulfilled aims, I am not aware that there is anything in the handling to which exception can be taken."

Nevertheless, *Jude the Obscure* was Hardy's last novel, for he concentrated on the writing of poetry after its publication and the criticism it evoked. It is, however, of great value both as art and document, for it enables the reader to enter imaginatively into the conventions, mores, and ways of thinking of an age removed from the present by less than three quarters of a century, but nevertheless an age holding to values which were perhaps ripe for Hardy's **satire**, and which reacted violently to that satire.

JUDE THE OBSCURE

TEXTUAL ANALYSIS

PART FIRST

Jude the Obscure is divided into six parts, each identified by the name of the places in Wessex, centering about the fictitiously-named university town of Christminster. Two of the six parts, in fact, are set in Christminster; Part Second, and Part Sixth. The parts are further divided into chapters which are untitled; there is a total of fifty-three chapters in this novel, numbered throughout each part of the six parts. Our detailed summary and analysis of the work will identify the chapters according to the sequence within the parts.

Part First ("At Marygreen"): Chapter One

The novel opens with a departure in a small village in Wessex, and a consequent change in the life of a little boy of eleven, whom we meet on the first page and who is to be the central figure in the novel. Jude Fawley. The man who is leaving is the village schoolmaster, Mr. Phillotson, and the author tells us that everybody in the village seemed sorry to see him leave. Phillotson is packing up such furniture and belongings as he owns for the move he is making to the city of Christminster, some twenty miles away. But the twenty miles, in rural England of the nineteenth century, and in the absence of good roads and rapid means of transportation, seems an enormous distance. The boy, Jude, feels that he will never see the schoolmaster, who has been his special friend, again, even though he is moving just this short distance.

Phillotson asks Jude, as they pack his goods on a small cart, whether he is sorry to see him leave, to which Jude replies what is in his heart: "yes." He is one of the few who begins to understand why the schoolmaster is leaving, for in some ways, as we shall see, Jude is intelligent and perceptive beyond his years. The schoolmaster is leaving for Christminster (actually Oxford), because he wishes to earn a university degree-as he tells Jude, it is "the necessary hallmark of a man who wants to do anything in teaching." Phillotson, in other words, plans to earn a degree (most schoolteachers in England at the time, of course, did not have university training), and then to be ordained a minister of the Church of England. Perhaps he plans to become the headmaster of a distinguished school; at any rate, he is ambitious for a better career in teaching, by means of the university and the Church, than he has at the beginning of the novel.

Phillotson's parting words, and even more, his example, sink deep into the consciousness of the young boy. Of Phillotson, Jude thinks: "He was too clever to bide here any longer." The village goes on in its narrow, even, unchanging, but tranquil way, much as it has in all probability done since the Middle Ages. Phillotson wants something better - and so does Jude.

Even as Phillotson leaves Marygreen, Jude is rudely recalled from a daydream about his ambitious teacher by the strident voice of his aunt, an old woman who is bringing up the orphaned Jude and who lives in a small cottage with Jude. Jude is ordered to go to the well, in the center of the village, and fetch two water buckets back to his aunt's cottage. The old lady, Drusilla Fawley, earns her living as a baker. As the first chapter closes, Jude arrives at the old well. This, "the only relic of the local history that remained absolutely unchanged," is to become a sort of symbol of permanence and stability, and is to be a contrast with the unrest and ultimately self-destructive ambition that is to torment Jude Fawley as he tries to pull himself up by study from the dead level of the little village.

Comment

Chapter One establishes the scene, in the small village or hamlet of Marygreen in North Wessex. More important, in very few words it gives us a clue to what the motivation of Jude will be throughout his life. He is inspired by the schoolmaster, Phillotson, to seek a kind of life which he believes is better than he can have at Marygreen. The university becomes Jude's ideal and his goal from this day; he wants to follow his teacher there. This chapter, and those which immediately follow it, comprise what in the terms of dramatic criticism is called the **exposition**, and Hardy is skillful in establishing in very few words and preliminary scenes the essence of his central character, Jude, and especially what is motivating him. Indeed, the entire novel is a study of the working-out of the ambition which the young Jude is presented as having acquired from Phillotson in the first chapter. And, as we shall see, while this ambition is in itself a praiseworthy thing - a man's wish to better himself beyond his surroundings - it is to be quite the wrong thing for Jude Fawley.

Part First: Chapter Two

As Chapter Two begins, Jude returns to great-aunt Drusilla's cottage with the two heavy water buckets; this is physical labor really beyond the boy's strength, but he is not one to complain. He finds himself listening to a conversation between his aunt and another elderly woman, Mrs. Williams and Drusilla tells the story of Jude and his parents to Mrs. Williams right in front of Jude. She seems rather outspoken, almost to the point of brutality, as she tells Mrs. Williams and other villagers about Jude. The "poor useless boy" has been living with her for a year; he came from Mellstock, in South Wessex, where he lived with his father until the latter died suddenly from "the shakings," and aunt Drusilla, as his closest surviving relative who could be responsible for his upbringing, took him in. But, at least in this scene, one gets the impression that Drusilla is not really glad to have the boy with her. Such is the tone of her remarks, and they are bound to cause some comment since they are made publicly.

Jude feels "the impact of their glances like slaps upon his face," as he sees his aunt and the other villagers possibly in their true attitude toward him for the first time. What his aunt says is bound to cause Jude to reflect on his parents, and it does, as we shall see. The story Drusilla tells is one of the tragic and untimely death of both of Jude's parents, after what was apparently a very unhappy marriage ending with their separation and then their death. She does not go into detail, but she warns Jude: "Jude, my child don't you ever marry. 'Tisn't for the Fawleys to take that step any more." As she tells the villagers as well as Jude something of the family history and its misfortunes, she also makes it known that Jude, like most of his family, is very much attracted to books. She wishes that the schoolmaster would have taken Jude off her hands and made a scholar of him in the university at Christminster, but this was not to be.

Two additional pieces of information given to the people by Drusilla are that Jude is earning a little towards his keep by working for Farmer Troutham scaring the birds away from the farmer's field ... yet even as she says this, Jude turns away, feeling the eyes of everyone on him. He is not to hold this position for very long. Also, the old woman mentions Jude's cousin, Sue, who had been born in Drusilla's own cottage, as having many of the same characteristics as Jude, especially her love of books.

Jude shrinks from all the attention, and as his aunt finishes by telling him never to marry, though for reasons unspecified, Jude goes out to the bakehouse and after having eaten his breakfast, makes his way to a large and lonely corn-field, which belongs to Farmer Troutham. He reflects on the place, while sounding a "clacker," which is a sort of rattle supposed to scare away the birds so that they will not eat the corn (actually wheat). Then, feeling sorry for the rooks-birds who are scavengers, similar to crows-he stops frightening them with the clacker. "His heart grew sympathetic with the birds' thwarted desires." Jude, in fact, feels a sense of identity with the birds, because nobody wants them, just as he feels that nobody wants him.

Just as Jude allows the birds to eat the grain, Farmer Troutham appears, and is infuriated at the boy, especially after hearing what Jude had said out loud to the birds. Jude tells him the truth, instead of denying everything as a born liar might have done - and the truth makes the farmer even more angry. He had hired Jude to watch the field, and instead the boy had invited the birds to dine. The farmer seizes Jude's rattle and beats him with it, and after the beating tells Jude, after giving him sixpence, never to be seen in his fields again. As he walks slowly away he weeps, from a sense that he had disgraced himself and not so much from the pain. Ironically, in the distance is heard the pealing of the bell of the church-tower, a building to which Farmer Troutham had contributed in its construction.

Jude returns, avoiding stepping on a number of earthworms. Hardy tells us that Jude was a boy who could not bear to hurt anything. He tells his aunt Drusilla that he is turned away from his job by the farmer, and shall have no more wages. She is really angry because she has "lost face" in the community, she fancies, by his coming, though she does not really care that he hadn't gotten along with the farmer, whose father after all had once worked for her father as his journeyman. The chapter ends as Drusilla tells Jude more about Christminster, and wishes out loud that he had gone there with the schoolmaster so that he would have been off her hands. Jude helps his aunt in her bakery shop the rest of the morning, and there being no more work to do, after plying her with more questions about Christminster, Jude goes into the village and, asking a man the directions to Christminster, sets out across the fields walking to find the city which has by now become the magical place of his dreams, which somehow, he seems to think, will rescue him from his unhappy situation if he can once go there.

Comment

This chapter continues the **exposition**, as we learn more about Jude's present situation, his character, and his parentage. Several things about him are of special importance, from the point of view of an explanation of his subsequent history and career.

In the first place, he is bookish, and this runs in his family. He is tender-hearted, being unwilling to hurt any living creature. These two things alone are in Hardy's view enough to bring him into conflict with his environment.

In addition, his parents were unhappily and indeed tragically married. Marriage is a state which does not seem to be beneficial to the Fawleys, and Jude is advised to avoid it, though telling an eleven-year-old boy such a thing will not make much of a conscious impression. It is as though the family is cursed, or such is the implication of what Jude's great-aunt Drusilla tells him. Also, the name of Sue, Jude's cousin, is raised for the first time here - and we learn from Drusilla that Sue has many of the same characteristics as Jude. Hardy's dramatic technique is especially notable in this chapter; he does not directly tell the reader anything much about Jude and his family history, but rather he has other characters tell what they know about the Fawleys. He also reveals character in action, as in the incident with Farmer Troutham. This dramatic, rather than narrative, progression, is one of the interesting aspects of the technique of *Jude the Obscure*, in general strengthening it as a work of fiction.

Part First: Chapter Three

As this chapter opens, the impression is created that Jude has been living in a very narrow and circumscribed environment- which indeed he has - but that now he is breaking loose somewhat from it. He climbs an old barn, and strains his eyes to see in the distance "the heavenly Jerusalem," Christminster, which has become his goal and aspiration much as the symbolic Jerusalem, the state of salvation, becomes the goal of the orthodox Christian. Indeed, the city of learning, Christminster, has become by this chapter a sort of substitute religion for Jude;

something in which he can put his faith. How his faith is repaid, Hardy will presently show us. But here, strain as he may, Jude cannot see the city. The difficulty Jude has in seeing the place is symbolic, to a certain extent. Jude prays, having re-ascended the ladder onto the roof of the barn, that he may be able to see the city. Finally, his efforts, natural or supernatural, are rewarded, for he is able just to make out the vanes, windows, slate roofs, and towers of Christminster. Suddenly, just as he has seen it, "the vague city became veiled in mist." As the sun goes down, the insubstantial pageant of Christminster vanishes into the mist, and dark shadows seem to appear to Jude, to take the city's place. As Jude goes homeward, he thinks of various myths and legends- one of them, involving Apollyon lying in wait for Christian, refers to John Bunyan's Pilgrim's Progress, in which Christian, who may represent suffering humanity seeking salvation, is waylaid by Apollyon, representing the powers of evil and darkness. If we accept even a mildly allegorical or symbolic reading of *Jude the Obscure*, Jude increasingly becomes a figure of Everyman - a symbol of all men, at least as Hardy saw them in his own age and society - who struggles toward an unattainable goal.

Hardy skillfully manipulates atmosphere and environment to reflect the moods of his central characters. Here in this scene, the reader may note the rain, the "sad wet season," in which Jude lives at this time, with nobody caring much about him. Jude eats his heart out with longing for what he imagines Christminster to be. After some days, it occurs to him that he could climb up on a building and see the night lights of Christminster. He sees them, and it seems to him that a message is carried to him by the bells of the famous university town. And the message is: "We are happy here."

Just as the entranced boy fancies that he hears this message of hope, a boy and a man appear with a coal-cart pulled by a team of horses. As they rest their team, Jude asks them if they have come from Christminster. They had not, but the carter has been there, and he tells Jude of the college life, as it appears to his unlearned eyes. In Christminster, he says, they are able to produce a "solemn preaching man with no corrupt passions." It is their business to turn out scholars and clergymen, and they do it well. There are men in the place who can "earn hundreds by thinking out loud." The carter has, in short, an uneducated man's awe at the mysteries of scholarship and severe study and he further whets the boy's appetite for study at Christminster by what he says. As the chapter concludes, Jude is even more strongly motivated, as he says to himself of the distant city: "It is what you may call a castle, manned by scholarship and religion." Finally, he observes: "It would just suit me."

Comment

This chapter has the function of reinforcing and making more plausible Jude's motivation to study at the university. Hardy does not state the motivation in so many words; he allows it to reveal itself slowly, in action and in the words of Jude himself. As we have already observed, Hardy's technique is dramatic; he shows a thing happening, and he does not spend much time directly telling the reader about it.

The university at Christminster, of course, represents an escape from his present unsatisfactory life, as well as more and more a substitute religion, for Jude. "It had been the yearning of his heart to find something to anchor on, to cling to-for some place which he could call admirable." Certainly his present surroundings are not in his view anything to be admired. As the chapter closes, he has definitely chosen Christminster as the city of his ideal.

Part First: Chapter Four

As Jude walks along, lost in thought, he meets up with a tall, rather fantastically-dressed man in a top hat, Physician Vilbert. Vilbert is known to him; he is a quack doctor who sells generally worthless remedies to the trusting and ignorant rural folk. It will be understood that a physician, especially one like this man, was more an object of suspicion than a respected healer to most people in the last century, certainly in the rural locale in which this novel is set - but in the absence of modern scientifically-derived medicine such a man traded on ignorance, fear, and greed. He, like the schoolmaster, Phillotson, is to become involved with Jude's life for a long time.

Jude questions Vilbert about Christminster, and the physician gives the impression that he is a university graduate. In all probability, he is lying about this too. He does, however, give the knowledge-hungry boy one accurate bit of information: that to learn Latin or Greek, the keys to entrance into the university at Christminster, he must get a grammar of each tongue. The doctor promises to sell to Jude the grammars he says he used as a student, if Jude will get some customers for Vilbert's patent medicines, his "golden ointment," his "life-drops," and other remedies, such as they are. For two weeks, Jude honestly performs his part of the bargain. He gives quite a number of orders for the medicines to Vilbert, who in turn has forgotten all about the grammars. No doubt he never had any intention of helping Jude in this matter, even if he could. Jude intuitively realizes that the physician is a dishonest man, whose word means nothing.

After going through a period of depression and blankness due to his realization of Vilbert's dishonesty, Jude has the idea of writing to Phillotson asking for the grammars, as he has no money of his own with which to buy them. He sends a note to Phillotson, and in due course the grammars come from Christminster. Jude had naively believed, in his ignorance, that a grammar would contain one all-embracing rule or formula by which one could translate one language into another. In this, as Hardy says, Jude is actually in advance of those who would be his teachers at Christminster, though he does not know this. There are linguistic laws, such as Grimm's law, which correspond to what Jude has imperfectly in mind. But when the grammars come from Phillotson, Jude is amazed and discouraged to find that, far from there being any general law for translation, each word of Greek and Latin must be individually committed to memory. He is really disillusioned now, and is prepared to give up his enterprise, even while recognizing that the scholars of the university must be even more intelligent than he had believed possible, to perform such prodigious feats of memory! Jude continues in a state of profound depression as the chapter ends.

Comment

This chapter brings Jude up against one aspect of human villainy: Physician Vilbert ("villain" - his name is significant). The physician takes advantage of and even worse, deliberately lies to a child, in return for a trifling profit. Jude is subconsciously made even more doubtful of human nature through his experience with the physician. But, on the positive side, Jude obtains his Latin and Greek grammars, and rather remarkably and commendably for a boy from an environment such as his, begins his studies which, he hopes, will lead him to the university at Christminster.

Part First: Chapter Five

Jude, during the next three or four years, applies himself to his studies, after getting over his initial discouragement. At the same time, he helps his aunt buy making deliveries of baked goods to the villagers around Marygreen in a horse and cart makeshift contraption he and his aunt have bought for the purpose. He reads from Caesar, Virgil, and Horace, often beholding the very spirit of the original, which Hardy tells us was "often to his mind something else than that which he was taught to look for." Jude studies while riding in the bakery cart, and because this is "different" in terms of the expectations of certain neighbors, he is ultimately cautioned by the local constable to look where he is going. But he perseveres in his studies, and makes progress which is really the more remarkable since he has no teacher, and must piece out the translations and points of grammar himself, with little or no possibility of checking his work to see if he is being accurate.

The scene by moonlight in this chapter in which Jude, moved by his surroundings to recite a Latin poem praising Diana, goddess of the moonlight, of hunting, and of chastity, is a significant turning point. "Potens Diana" - powerful Diana - is, after all, a pagan goddess, and this is a profane (as opposed to a sacred) work. But Jude's ambition, which would be realized only by his admission to the University, is to become not only a classical scholar, but a clergyman as well. And profane learning does not fit well with this object. He resolves to change the material of his study. Therefore, he turns to the New Testament in Greek, especially to the Gospels: Matthew, Mark, Luke, and John, and to the Epistles. He also reads the Church Fathers; the great writers of the early days of Christianity, who by and large Hardy thought, were ascetics in that they denied the power of the flesh and of man's animal passions, and tried to subdue these. This distinction will be important as we shall soon see the conflict between flesh and spirit in which Jude is to become involved in the next chapter.

While he reads the Church Fathers, such as St. Jerome and St. Augustine, he gets the idea that he needs a congenial trade so that he will be able to make a living while studying at Christminster. He decides that he can become a stonemason, especially after he spends time reading the Latin inscriptions in the local churchyards. The university town is, after all, filled with great works of stone, and these will be in need of repair, Jude is sure. As the chapter ends, Jude is nineteen, and now a stonemason and stonecutter with some knowledge of Greek and Latin, rather remarkable under the circumstances of his environment. But he still does not know the world and, as Hardy would imply, the possibilities of wickedness therein; his arduous self-education has already made him learned, but not shrewd or calculating. This is an undoubted virtue of character in Jude, especially as Hardy develops this character through self-revealing action. But it is not a strength which will enable Jude to cope with the world.

Comment

This chapter advances the action. It is filled with **irony**, in that Jude is reading books of religious wisdom, especially the Gospels and the ascetic Church Fathers, at this time. Very shortly, his scholarly ambitions and interests and the instincts of the flesh will come into brutal collision, and this will take place in the next chapter. Hardy prepares the way for a confrontation of the young would-be scholar and clergyman with the flesh.

Part First: Chapter Six

One Saturday, a brilliant summer afternoon, Jude is returning from Alfredston to Marygreen. By chance - the kind of coincidence upon which Hardy so often relies in his fiction - he goes by a roundabout way. He reviews in his mind some of his educational achievements, and finds them pleasing to him; he takes pride in these, and indulges in a daydream. While it is true, as he tells himself, that he had "acquired quite an average student's power to read the common ancient classics, Latin in particular," and while we as the readers recognize that Jude's achievement is the more remarkable because it has been by the young man on his own, without a teacher - yet his dreams do not seem in accordance with reality. He will, he tells himself, "be D.D. before I have done." He expects to become a Doctor of Divinity, and to have the social and financial position that a high-ranking churchman of the Church of England would have had in English society of the nineteenth century.

But even as Jude dreams of a career in learning and in the church, reality obtrudes. From the other side of a hedge, he hears the voices of some girls, though he cannot see the originators of these sounds. Suddenly something smacks him on the ear - a cold soft substance. It is a part of a male pig, in fact the genital organs, and Jude, wanting to know who has so crudely thrown such an object at him, looks over the fence by the hedge. On the other side, he sees three young women washing pigs' chitterlings in the clean brook, no doubt preparing them for sale. Next to where they work is a small house, with a garden and pigsties.

Jude speaks severely to the girls, but they deny, each in turn, having thrown the offal at him. One of them, however, catches his attention - "a fine dark-eyed girl" who has more than a trace of animalism about her. Jude instinctively singles her out from among the three, and she looks closely at him. Already they have some kind of an affinity for each other, and something which is not at all rational. Jude learns that the girl's name is Arabella Donn, and that her father raises pigs for a living. Arabella, in fact, herself has many aspects of the animal about her. Commentators about this novel have sometimes referred to her as the pig-girl or the pig-woman who entraps Jude through an appeal to his animal nature. For Jude, she does indeed have a fatal and magnetic attraction, almost entirely sexual. This is the first time that the nineteen year-old Jude has looked at a woman as a woman. Unfortunately for him, he has looked at the wrong woman, and he realizes this very intellectually. Her coarseness and lack of shame is symbolized by what she throws at him to attract his attention at their first chance meeting. He knows that she will be a distraction, if not worse.

But somehow Jude cannot help himself, even though he knows better. He knows, for example, that it was no innocent girl who threw that object at him. But he cannot act on this knowledge. Instead, he makes a date to call upon her the next Sunday. The other two girls imply in their talk with Arabella after Jude leaves that she is trying to snare him, and that he is very innocent, judging by the way he looked at her. But she denies this.

Comment

Jude shows himself here as weak-as one who knows what he should do, but is too weak to act on his knowledge that the girl Arabella is not good enough for him and that if he gets involved with her it will be his misfortune. The basic dualism - the warfare between the weak flesh and the aspiring spirit which Hardy represented in the character of Jude-is here embodied, so that this Chapter occupies a key place in the first part of *Jude the Obscure*. The conflict within Jude himself, which will occupy much of the book, is set forth against the dark background of fate which has been hinted at earlier in regard to Jude's family. The Fawleys are unlucky in marriage and in relations with women. Jude, as we begin to see here, is to be no exception.

Here, then, may be another meaning of the complete title of the book, including "the Obscure." Jude's motives are obscure to himself; he has little real insight into what he is doing, though he does have some intellectual understanding. To the modern reader, especially one with even the most elementary lay knowledge of the doctrines of modern psychology, Jude's behavior is not so obscure. Jude desires the girl Arabella, even though she is likely to be very bad for him. His desire leads to his fate, and his fate is to be such that though he is one of the obscure millions of the world, living and dying unwept and unhonored, yet Hardy implies that his life and death, by their meaning, rise from obscurity to challenge the very justice of the heavens themselves.

Part First: Chapter Seven

The following Sunday after his initial meeting with Arabella, Jude tries to do what he knows to be the sensible thing: to break his date with her. Instead, he sits down with the Greek text of the New Testament, and begins to read; the Greek is from II Corinthians, Chapter 3, verse 14: "But their minds were blinded ... ." Hardy, of course, cannot resist this ironic touch. Jude's mind is blinded, as we have seen in the previous chapter. "A compelling arm of extraordinary muscular power" seizes Jude, as he tells himself that he will not go visit Arabella after all, and he forgets his good intention and leaves his studies. He tells himself that he feels sorry for the girl, waiting as she will be for someone who will never come. But this is a rationalization.

Reaching Arabella's house, he smells the piggeries. But soon he is waking out with her, towards the Brown House from which he had beheld Christminster in the distance: But Christminster is forgotten now, as are Diana, Phoebus Apollo, the Latin and Greek classics, and Jude's ambitions to be a D.D., bishop, and professor. Jude and Arabella walk further than they, or at any rate Jude, had planned. When they stop, it is at an inn, or public house, which has inside on the wall the significant and ironic picture of Samson and Delilah. Jude, of course, like Samson, is about to be robbed of his strength and freedom by a designing women. And Arabella is certainly that; for a presumably innocent young girl, she knows a suspicious amount about beer, liquor, and public houses. After drinking some beer, she and Jude leave and walk home arm in arm. They are now lovers, or so says Arabella. Jude had intended to be back at his Greek studies at 3:30 in the afternoon, but somehow he finds that it is not until 9:00 in the evening that he returns Arabella home.

Jude's Greek is forgotten. His books remain unread, while his wishes are no longer directed to learning, but toward Arabella and his desire for her. Meanwhile, she discusses the affair with Anny and Sarah, her two cronies who had originally been with her on the day she met Jude. Arabella tells them that she wishes to marry Jude, and they suggest, in effect, that she should take advantage of his innocence of the world and its ways. She is to use the oldest ruse of all: seduction, and a forced marriage. Only it will be Arabella, of course, who is the seductress, the temptress, even though Jude will blame himself for everything, being that way inclined.

Comment

This chapter shows the weakness of Jude when he is confronted by the demands of the flesh. What Arabella trusts in is, paradoxically, Jude's essential innocence and what Hardy implies is his decency. She would not plan what she does if she believed Jude to be other than honest. In other words, like Samson himself, Jude will be shorn of his freedom by a woman, through his very strength and honesty. This is the paradoxical nature of his character and his life, at least as Hardy presents them for his own symbolic purposes.

Part First: Chapter Eight

One weekend soon after the above meeting, Jude visits Arabella, and rather by accident or coincidence, a favorite Hardy fictional device, they meet even though Jude didn't intend a meeting. As he sees her, she is chasing several young pigs who had escaped from their sty. Nobody is home but Arabella and the pigs, and as she pursues the pigs-symbols of her animalism from which Jude is unable to rescue himself-Jude catches her. Very cleverly, she leads him on, and really plays cat and mouse with him, even while he tells himself that perhaps he is taking too much liberty with her. As this scene ends, Jude has Arabella even more on his mind, and his Greek books remain unread. Soon comes a Sunday on which Jude visits Arabella, and, the rest of the family being out, she invites him to come in for tea. She holds a cochin's egg in her bosom, and by telling him not to touch her as it might break, she lures him closer. Of course, given what we can now see as Jude's lack of self-control, artfully played upon by Arabella, it is no surprise that Jude allows himself to be carried away by passion, and Hardy makes it quite clear, as he constructs the scene, that Jude is motivated simply by physical desire for

Arabella. Hardy follows the **conventions** of the Victorian novel in not describing scenes of seduction in detail, but we are led by him to assume that Jude is not really the aggressor here: that he has been led on by Arabella.

Comment

Here Jude is deflected from his ambitions toward learning and a career in the Church by rather crude physical desire, based in part on sheer ignorance and aroused by a girl who is not really worthy of him. This chapter establishes clearly, however, that Jude does know what he is doing, and his seduction of Arabella-or more accurately her seduction of him so that he will marry her-will be his downfall, though it means much less to her. She probably likes Jude as much as she can like anyone, for she is so selfish. But her feeling for him cannot be described as love, nor can the desire he feels for her be so described in any higher terms. Principally Arabella sees Judes as an escape from her drab surroundings and her unsatisfactory life as a keeper of pigs. But a wish to escape from something is hardly a basis for an enduring marriage relationship. Hardy becomes rather unpleasantly detailed in describing the circumstances and surroundings of her life, but his purpose is to show us at least part of her motivation to marry Jude.

Part First: Chapter Nine

Two months after the encounter of Jude and Arabella, Jude tells her that he now plans to go away and begin his career at Christminster. It is never too late to mend, he says. Meanwhile, she seems more and more uneasy. She consults the quack doctor, Physician Vilbert, and while we are not told what information she obtains from him, a good guess would be that he tells her how to deceive Jude further. Thus, upon hearing Jude say that he is going to break off their relationship, she tells him, with all the circumlocution characteristic of the Victorian novel, that she is pregnant with his child. A quick and forced marriage is indicated, and Jude agrees to marry Arabella. Again, she trades on his essential innocence. He knows that the marriage is a mistake, but wishes to do the honorable thing. "His idea of her was the thing of most consequence, not Arabella herself, he sometimes said laconically." That is, he further deludes himself into believing that Arabella is the right person for him to marry.

Arabella's parents, the parson, and the country folk generally suspect that this is a forced marriage, but approve of it as is the local custom. So the marriage takes place before the parson, and Hardy describes it in these rather cynical terms: "And so, standing before the aforesaid officiator, the two swore that at every other time of their lives they would assuredly believe, feel, and desire precisely as they had believed, felt, and desired during the few preceding weeks. What was as remarkable as the undertaking itself was the fact that nobody seemed at all surprised at what they swore." Her we find the first important indication of one of the three objects of Hardy's **satire** of the institutions in his society in *Jude the Obscure*: the institution of marriage, not necessarily in itself, but as it was observed, in Hardy's view, in the latter part of the nineteenth century in Victorian England.

At his marriage, Jude's financial prospects are poor. He is nineteen. As an apprentice stone-mason, he will receive only half-wages until he completes his apprenticeship, which customarily was a period of seven years. He takes a small cottage where Arabella can have a garden and perhaps keep a few pigs, as she waits for the expected child. If she married him in order to escape her unsatisfactory home life, she is no better off than she had been previously!

But there is no child, and Jude learns that she had been "mistaken" about the pregnancy which caused him to marry her. He also learns other things about her, which give him even less respect for her character. She has been a barmaid, which was not an exalted occupation in that society and locale. This Jude hadn't known, or he would have been less disposed to believe in her innocence. Indeed, when she tells him that their forced marriage was unnecessary, he is almost struck dumb with surprise. Now he realizes how he has been tricked. He has, for a time, "no more to say," he is so stunned by the news. The discovery that she even wears a wig, a "long tail of hair, which Arabella wore twisted up in an enormous knob at the back of her head," is just one more symbolic manifestation to Jude of Arabella's falsity, which subconsciously he had known all along, Hardy implies. While Jude had married as the result of a mistake, or more plainly, an outright lie on Arabella's part, what is done cannot be undone, and the marriage remained.

Comment

With this chapter, we begin to see one of the satirical topics or thematic strands of this novel: the **satire** of the institution of marriage. Hardy will, as has been pointed out, choose three inter-related social institutions for the objects of his satire:

1. Marriage

2. Education

3. Religion

More accurately, he will satirize and attack what he, Hardy, saw as the abuses inherent in these institutions in his society. Whether we agree with his vision, given the changes in laws, customs, and institutions in the past three quarters of a century since *Jude the Obscure* was written, we must at least consider the honesty of his attempt to portray a state of affairs in which the formalism of empty institutions, in his view, militated against the freedom and power of self-development of the members of his society, whether great or, like Jude, "obscure."

Part First: Chapter Ten

This chapter seems rather unrelated to those which immediately precede it, and in terms of the kind of action involved, it is. But in terms of thematic significance and characterization - the further characterization of both Jude and Arabella - it is highly relevant. All that happens, outwardly, is the slaughtering of a pig by Jude. Challow, the man whose employment it is to kill pigs in Marygreen, is supposed to come to kill the young couple's pig, which they have been raising for the meat. But as the butcher does not come on time, Jude is forced, against his will, to slaughter the pig himself-since the pig is starving and they have run out of feed for it.

"Pigs must be killed," says Arabella, as the pig expires agonizingly. But to Jude, it is "a hateful business!" Arabella catches the last of the pig's blood in a vessel, as she has a use in her household for almost every part of the animal. Jude is praised for the way that he slaughtered the pig by Mr. Challow, who arrives just as the pig breathes its last. But he loathes what he has done, even while Arabella is utterly cold and unemotional about it. Indeed, there is a reversal of traditional male-female roles here, with Arabella being the hard-hearted one. The slaughtering is very graphically presented, even by contemporary standards of description, and the account may seem needlessly bloody. But Hardy does this for a purpose, as we shall see.

The second part of Chapter Ten, by a rather clumsy use of coincidence, involves Jude's discovery as to the way in which Arabella entrapped him. For as he goes along the road to Alfredston soon after the affair of the pig, he hears voices by the stream near where he had first met Arabella. Indeed, he overhears a conversation between the two girls who had been Arabella's companions on that very day when he met her - and further, they happen to be engaging in gossip about Jude and Arabella just as Jude is, unknown to them, passing by. "Howsomever, 'twas I put her up to it!" one of them says to the other. While the rest of the conversation is not heard by Jude, he has heard enough to know the full extent of Arabella's trickery.

When he finally reaches home, determined to guard his tongue so that he will not start a flight with Arabella over what he has heard and believed, Arabella is unusually talkative. She wants some money. He tells her that an apprentice does not really earn sufficient money on which to marry, as she well knew. She persists - so he tells her something of what her "women friends" had said.

Very coldly, she replies: "Every woman has a right to do such as that. The risk is hers." He disputes this, and begins to call into question the very nature of their marriage relationship, which in his view can become permanent bondage as a result of temporary weakness. As the chapter closes, Arabella, rather significantly, continues melting down some pig fat, unmoved by her task or by what Jude has been saying.

Comment

The slaughter of the pig is symbolic of what Jude elsewhere in the novel calls "Nature's law of mutual butchery." The action tends to establish Jude's character further as tender-hearted and unwilling to hurt any living thing, man, woman, or beast. It is this characteristic, plus his temporary loss of control over his passions, which had entrapped him into marriage with Arabella. Hardy so bloodily describes the killing of the pig in an attempt to shock the reader into seeing beneath the surface of reality into the jungle world of conflict, selfishness, and callous indifference to suffering which he sees as existing in hidden fashion in his society.

Arabella's reactions both to the killing of the pig and to Jude's revelation that he has overheard her girl acquaintances talking about her plot against him are quite revealing also. Arabella is unmoved and unemotional. "Pigs must be killed." Yes, and a woman such as herself has the right to lie to her prospective husband and feel no shame at the lie, for Nature's law knows no honor or tenderness. Such is her view, at any rate, and the really significant aspect of this presentation of such a character by Hardy is the ultimate outcome of her life as compared with that of Jude.

Part First: Chapter Eleven

The following Sunday, Arabella continues melting down the pig's fat, in part because subconsciously she seems to know that this antagonizes her husband, who does not even like to be reminded of the slaughter of the pig. In turn, this precipitates a serious quarrel: Arabella starts to throw some of Jude's classical books off the table onto the floor, meanwhile smearing them with the hot grease with which her hands are covered as a result of boiling down the pig-fat. Jude is infuriated, as this wanton action probably symbolizes to him the mess into which he has fallen as a result of his hasty marriage. Jude uses physical force against her to make her promise to leave the books alone, and she desists and goes out on the highway.

Here she walks up and down in a distraught manner, shouting to all who pass by that Sunday morning on the way to church that her husband is ill-treating her; she claims that he is forcing her to work on Sundays instead of allowing her to attend church, and she further says that he has been tearing her hair off her head and ripping her dress. All of these are lies, of course; it was Arabella who began the quarrel, not Jude. Jude is about to go out after her, exasperated, and pull her in by force, when he suddenly loses interest. "Their lives were ruined, he thought; ruined by the fundamental error of their matrimonial union; that of having based a permanent contract on a temporary feeling… ." From this point, the reader also realizes that the marriage between Arabella and Jude is at the point of breaking up. Arabella adds fuel to the fire as she throws up to him the past marital histories of his family: how his father ill-used his mother, and his father's sister ill-used her husband. Jude is surprised at this talk, and, leaving the cottage, goes to his great-Aunt Drusilla at Marygreen. He asks her whether what Arabella had said was true, and learns that substantially it was all true. Jude's father and mother couldn't get on with each other, and separated after his birth-left one another on the hill by the Brown house, in fact. His mother drowned herself soon after the separation. And it was the same with Jude's father's sister. "The Fawleys were not made for wedlock … There's sommat in our blood that won't take kindly to the notion of being bound to do what we do readily enough if not bound." Drusilla has said this before to the boy, but now he is a man and married, she repeats the thought with added fore. Jude should never have married.

By the Brown house that evening he comes near the frozen pond there and goes out onto the treacherous ice, hoping that it will break through so that he will drown and thus end his troubles. But "peaceful death abhorred him as a subject and would not take him." He is not in his own eyes sufficiently dignified to end his life in this manner, and the ice will not crack. Instead, he decides to get drunk. In all this, he behaves as a most immature character, but we know what is motivating his actions. As he arrives back home that evening drunk, he finds, not Arabella, but a note: "Have gone to my friends. Shall not return."

Several days later, Jude receives a letter from his wife telling him that she is planning to emigrate to Australia with her parents, as she sees no chance of bettering herself ever if she remains with Jude. Here we have confirmation of the strong suspicion that Arabella only married Jude as an escape, and seeing that she had escaped nothing by the marriage, broke it up at the first opportunity. She is, in short, as selfish as a pig. Jude writes back saying that perhaps this decision of Arabella's is for the best. He helps to arrange an auction of even the meager furniture of their house, sending the furniture over to the house of Arabella's parents because their goods are also being auctioned. He includes his own framed portrait, which he had himself inscribed "Jude to Arabella" on the back and given it to Arabella on their marriage.

When he sees that Arabella has even had his portrait auctioned off with the rest of the household goods, for one shilling, he realizes that she doesn't care for him at all and probably never has had the slightest feeling for him. He buys the portrait and burns it, frame and all, in his lodgings, as sign that the relationship is absolutely finished. Then, passing by the place where the parting between his own father and mother was thought to have taken place, he suddenly turns his mind back to his dreams of the university at Christminster. On a milestone in the direction of that city he reads, by the light of a match, what he himself had cut into the stone years ago: "Thither" and his initials, "J.F." As the chapter, and the first or introductory section of the novel, end, Jude has once more resolved to go to Christminster. He will do this as soon as his apprenticeship expires. And he will try to forget the unhappiness which had come about through his marriage to Arabella.

Comment

Hardy has set things up so that the reader is not exactly surprised at the disintegration of Jude's marriage with Arabella. It had been founded on sand: on deception and physical entrapment on her part, and Arabella was much too coarse to be compatible with Jude. This chapter, therefore, pulls together the action of the Part First, which is in a sense Jude's growth to the estate of manhood.

Jude the Obscure may be described as a Bildungsroman, or novel of development - a fictional form popular in the nineteenth and even the twentieth centuries in England, on the Continent, and in the United States. Goethe's *Sorrows of Young Werther* is perhaps the most famous example of the novel of development, but others, more recent, such as Maugham's *Of Human Bondage*, Samuel Butler's *The Way of All Flesh*, and James Joyce's *A Portrait of the Artist as a Young Man*, the latter being probably the most famous in this form in our century in English - all of these have in common the subject of the development of a young man from the storms and stresses of youth and adolescence into manhood. More often than not, the period of youth is a severe trial, but the books end happily in that the young man learns at the end what he needs to learn about life and about himself in order to survive and to live satisfactorily. The young hero of the novel of development - the three heroes of the last three books mentioned above, for example: Philip Carey of *Human Bondage*, Ernest Pontifex of *The Way of All Flesh*, and Stephen Dedalus of *A Portrait of the Artist as a Young Man*, all are stronger and more developed characters as the books end. They are ready to face life.

But *Jude the Obscure* reverses the pattern. Jude is hopeful, having suffered in his youth, that he can survive and somehow improve himself. Even if his fate seems to be unhappiness, he is, at the end of Part First of the novel, still prepared to do battle with this fate and out of disaster pluck strength and safety. At the end of Part First, Jude still has hope. He has suffered, but he is young and resilient, and is ready to fight. The question in our mind, as we turn to the second part of the book, is whether Jude will be able to maintain that hope, and whether he will so easily be able to escape the disastrous marriage into which he had so unwisely entered.

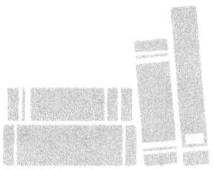

JUDE THE OBSCURE

TEXTUAL ANALYSIS

PART SECOND

Part Second ("At Christminster"): Chapter One

With this chapter begins Jude's attempt to find a new life, free of the mistakes of his early youth, in the city of his dreams, Christminster. He has waited years for the moment when he approaches Christminster ... but, as we will presently see, just as Part First ended with a disaster and a break with an area on the part of Jude, so Part Second will end. "It is better to journey hopefully than to arrive" reads an old Japanese proverb, expressing a universal thought. Jude, at this point in his life, does indeed journey, but as he approaches Christminster for the first time, it is clear from all that has gone before that his journey and his expectation are hopeful. The question is whether or not he will maintain this hopefulness.

There is a three year gap between the parting of Jude and Arabella at the end of Part First, and the scene which we discover at the start of this chapter. The locale is, of course, Christminster, or the approaches leading to that city; Jude is traveling the road into Christminster after having served out his time as an apprentice stone-mason in Marygreen and Alfredston. He is now twenty-two years old, has been married and separated, though apparently not divorced from Arabella (for divorce was difficult and financially expensive in Victorian England, requiring an Act of Parliament which would have been far beyond the financial means of one in Jude's humble circumstances). He and Arabella, then, have simply parted, and this fact will be important later in the novel. Hardy provides us with a description of Jude as he enters Christminster: he is younger than he looks now, as he wears a thick but closely-trimmed beard and his face looks out at the world under a mass of curly black hair. He has become an expert, having passed beyond his apprentice and journeyman stages, in monumental stone-cutting, including the repair of churches, and stone-carving.

Jude walks the last four miles into Christminster from choice, rather than necessity. Possibly he thinks of himself as a pilgrim humbly entering the temple of learning - and a pilgrim might well be traveling on foot. But it is significant that the "ultimate impulse," as Hardy calls it, for Jude to come to Christminster, was emotional and not intellectual. Jude had seen, at his Aunt Drusilla's house in Marygreen, the photograph of a pretty young girl. Her name is Sue Bridehead, and she is Jude's cousin. Aunt Drusilla does not know where she lives, except that it is in Christminster, and she refuses to give Jude the photograph- we gather that she has reservations about the girl, and about Jude's meeting her. But this quickened Jude's desire to go to Christminster. As he arrives, Hardy pictures him as "a species of Dick Whittington." Now Dick Whittington is a sort of English Horatio Alger, a young penniless boy without family who comes, according to legend, to London and by hard work and luck becomes "thrice Lord Mayor of London." The tableau or scene on the road outside Christminster forms a parallel with the legend of Dick Whittington. But it is to be an ironic parallel. What of the Dick Whittingtons who come to their particular and fated town or city, and instead of becoming great successes, simply move from obscurity into obscurity and nothingness? This is the question Hardy poses in *Jude the Obscure*.

Jude finds a lodging-house and takes a room. Immediately he explores Christminster, especially one of the colleges, at least from the outside. It is late at night, and he seems to feel the unseen but real presence of the illustrious scholars and religious leaders and statesmen who had been nurtured by the college- clearly one of the Oxford colleges. None of the men is named, but all would have been known to Hardy's contemporary reader: Cardinal Newman; Matthew Arnold, the great English poet and literary critic; Edward Gibbon; Edward Pusey, one of the Tractarians or religious reformers in Oxford of the group known as the Oxford Movement in the latter part of the nineteenth century. The clergymen associated with this particular college (actually Oriel College, Oxford), especially interest Jude, for the Church is the goal of his professional and scholarly ambition, as we have seen. Jude is enraptured, and even begins talking to himself - and a policeman asks him just what he thinks he is doing there. Jude therefore goes home, but not before the ringing words of several oddly-contrasted great graduates of the college pass through his mind: the skeptical words of the historian Gibbon; the optimism of the poet, Arnold ("How the world is made for each of us!"); the piety of Newman, the author of the Apologia, writing of "the absolute certitude as to the truths of natural theology." This is a procession of greatness, though of men who attained to radically differing intellectual positions about religious matters especially. Jude muses about them until he falls asleep, still dreaming of them. When he wakes, he remembers that he is going to meet his young cousin,

Sue, and also Phillotson, his old schoolmaster who had fired him with the wish to come to Christminster and who had mailed him the Latin and Greek grammars so many years previously.

Comment

This chapter serves as the transition from Jude's boyhood and young manhood in Marygreen to his life in what has become his own New Jerusalem, Christminster. Now he is in the city of his ambitions and dreams, and he starts out humbly, worshipping the very stones of which the city is built-for all are filled with memories of greatness in the sphere of the intellect and of piety. The great men who symbolize the place for Jude are interesting from the point of view of the social and intellectual background of the novel-for they were men who, whatever their undoubted brilliance and sincerity, came to very different conclusions about the fundamental questions troubling Hardy's age: the validity of orthodox Christianity, the duty of man in this life, and the possibility of human immortality. These questions are also of concern to Jude-he wishes to find answers to some of them in Christminster. And he hopes to find his old schoolmaster, now, he thinks, a successful dignitary of the Church. Judging from the tone of the novel so far, we are rather skeptical of Jude's success in his endeavors in Christminster, though his sincerity is touching, as Hardy meant it to be.

Part Second: Chapter Two

Jude must solve the "mean bread-and-cheese question," by which Hardy means that he must find work in order to make a living. Jude at first seeks to work with a group of stone-masons who are repairing some of the buildings of the university, crumbling with age. Unfortunately, Jude does not succeed in obtaining employment in the stonecutter's yard right away, and as he waits to see what he can do in Christminster, he speculates on the meaning of the architecture he sees. Hardy comments of Jude: "He did not at that time see that medievalism was as dead as a fern-leaf in a lump of coal; that other developments were shaping in the world around him, in which Gothic architecture and its associations had no place. The deadly animosity of contemporary logic and vision towards so much of what he held in reverence was not yet revealed to him." By this is implied that what Jude has placed his faith in: the Church, and Oxford as the symbol and intellectual center at least of the English Church, is moribund in Jude's century; it has no chance for its proper influence on the life of the world, in view of this "deadly animosity." This point is important, because it leads into the second major object of Hardy's social criticism in *Jude the Obscure*: the Church and orthodox Christianity, which is to become increasingly irrelevant to Jude's situation. "Gothic" architecture, like "Gothic" religion, belongs to medieval times, but Jude has not yet realized this fact.

For a number of days, Jude simply wanders around the colleges of Christminster seeing what they are like. He feels himself to be a part of them by virtue of his study and desire for learning. But as he will find, he is still an "outsider" in all senses of the term. To fill in time, he thinks of his cousin Sue; what sort of person is she? he asks himself. He prevails upon his reluctant aunt to send him Sue's picture, and she does this while cautioning him again not to go to see the girl. Apparently Aunt Drusilla knows that the worst will happen, in view of the "fate" of the Fawley family regarding marriage.

Jude sees and rubs shoulders with some of the college students, but "he was as far from them as if he had been at the antipodes." This is because he is dressed as a workman, and in the rigidly class-structured society in which he finds himself, he has even less chance than he himself thinks to become a university student. But finally Jude receives the offer of employment at the stonemason's yard, and promptly accepts it. Buying a few books, and renting a small room, he determines to study by night and work by day, and to save his wage against the time when he can apply for admission to the university. Meanwhile, he learns that Sue is working for a firm which sells ecclesiastical supplies: prayerbooks, texts, Bibles, etc. The place seems, when Jude visits it, to be High-Church Anglican - that is, in some way related to that part of the Church of England which, as Jude says to himself, is close to Roman Catholicism in many of its rituals. Jude himself doesn't seem to care for such distinctions, but his Aunt Drusilla was a member of an Evangelical Protestant sect, and thus would have been even more suspicious, on religious grounds, of Sue.

Significantly, when Jude walks into the place where Sue is employed, his first sight of her is brought about as he sees her designing, on four-foot long scroll made of zinc, the ornamented letters, Alleluia, which is of course from the Hebrew ("praise ye the Lord"). Again, this first sight of the person with whom Jude's fate is to be so closely linked is treated by Hardy with some measure of irony.

Jude does not speak to Sue at first; he simply observes her and returns several times in the course of the next two or three weeks. He does see her by accident one day while he is at work at one of the colleges, and it occurs to him that her years of life in London must have rubbed some of the country rawness off her. This realization makes him even more eager to make himself known to her, even despite the bars to his doing this: he is married, and he and Sue are cousins-both good reasons why he should not see her. As the chapter ends, he is undecided, but we strongly suspect that he will not be able to resist the wish to see Sue.

Comment

This chapter shows Jude as holding some beliefs: in the lofty purpose of the university of Christ minster, in the Church, and even in architecture, which Hardy thought of as outmoded. Jude still does not realize the nature of the world in which he is living. He also deceives himself about the source of his interest in his cousin Sue. Although he rationalizes this, the truth is that at a distance, after seeing her picture, he finds himself falling involve with his cousin, and this is intensified when he actually sees her. But there remain signs of implications that if he once meets her, the result may well be disaster.

Part Second: Chapter Three

Jude attends the next Sunday service at the church of one of the colleges, principally because he hopes to see Sue there since he knows that she frequently attends this service. He waits all morning, and into the afternoon, when she finally arrives. He follows her into the building, but still does not reveal himself to her.

As the choir sings a psalm: "Wherewithal shall a young man cleanse his way? Jude reflects on his previous behavior and accuses himself in his own mind of various sins: animal passion, attempted suicide, drunkenness. The choice of the psalm on Hardy's part is, of course, another bit of irony-because

Jude's motivation to see Sue is far from spiritual, whatever he may tell himself. Hardy makes that quite clear. "He could not altogether be blind to the real nature of the magnetism." By means of a flashback, the reader is made aware of a walk Sue had, just previous to this time, taken in the country with a book. On impulse, she had purchased from a swarthy foreigner-not knowing exactly what made her do this-two plaster statues which were copies of ancient Greek statues. She buys the statues of Venus and Apollo, of course the embodiments respectively of female and male physical beauty.

After she has paid her few shillings for the statues, and carried them away, she realizes what she has done: they are quite naked, and she covers them with leaves. Her landlady, Miss Fontover, the daughter of a clergyman, calls on Sue and shows interest in the statues. Because of their nature, Sue feels obliged to equivocate about them to the rather nosy old lady, and says that they are religious statues: St. Peter and St. Mary Magdalene. In the presence of the statues, in her room, Sue then begins reading a book which she has kept carefully hidden from her landlady, who of course would not approve of it: Gibson's Decline and Fall of the Roman Empire. Gibbon, of course, was skeptical in matters of religion, and therefore was not considered to be quite proper for someone like Sue to read; certainly not the chapter on the reign of Julian the Apostate. As Sue reads Gibbon, Jude is at the same time reading his Greek New Testament in his own room.

Comment

This chapter is filled with material objects as well as the actions of Sue and Jude which carry symbolic meaning. The statues of pagan deities, bought by Sue in a way against her better judgment, symbolize the conflict in her between the rational and the emotional side of her nature, the latter having been apparently starved for expression. Jude's visit to the church is likewise motivated by unconscious forces: he wants to see Sue, and he comes to desire her, even as he tells himself that he is interested only in her well-being. And even as he reflects on his heretofore disastrous relationship with Arabella, he is preparing new trouble for himself.

Part Second: Chapter Four

This chapter finally sees the meeting face-to-face of Sue Bridehead and Jude Fawley. As Jude's resistance to such a meeting diminishes the more he thinks about Sue, another bit of knowledge is just on the point of presenting itself to Jude which will further weaken his self-determination with regard to Sue, and will also make him doubt the possibility of his ever achieving a career in scholarship and in the Church. Jude is in the understandable situation of wanting something to love. It may be said that up until this time the only object Jude ever loved was not even a person, but an idea: the idea of Christminster and the spirit of impartial and disinterested scholarship with which Jude had been burning ever since first got the idea, as a small boy, from his hero the schoolmaster Phillotson.

He is therefore fixing his thoughts on Sue, but still has the vision of Christminster in his mind somewhat to counterbalance his attraction to Sue. Having been "burned once" by Arabella, he knows both intellectually and by experience that if he gives in to what he is beginning to feel for Sue he will inevitably suffer, and this time probably be ruined completely. "From his own orthodox point of view," Hardy says of Jude, "the situation was growing immoral." He is by the laws of England - the matrimonial bond-licensed ... to love Arabella and none other unto his life's end." This Hardy says ironically, making clear his own belief that the marriage laws of his day were destructively rigid.

Jude goes so far as to pray against the weakness, but this is not a valid remedy for him, and he still cannot outgrow or be free from the temptation represented by Sue.

Meanwhile, Sue comes to visit Jude at work. He is not there, but later one of the men tells him of Sue's visit, and he recognizes who his visitor was, though she has not left her name. She sends a note to his lodgings, and asks to meet him, at the same time telling him that she is soon to go away. He is afraid now that he may not see her for very long and that he has delayed seeing her until it was really too late. They arrange to meet at dusk, "at the cross in the pavement which marked the spot of the martyrdoms." And they do meet, but Sue says that they should walk further on before coming any closer - a symbolic action. "I am not going to meet you just there," she says, because of the association of the spot with suffering.

Jude admits at their meeting that he knows her better than she knows him. She in turn casually gives him what to him is a most shocking piece of news: simply that Phillotson - the same Richard Phillotson who had been his schoolteacher - is now a country-schoolmaster at Lumsdon, a small town or village a little way outside Christminster. He is profoundly depressed at the news, and upon meeting Phillotson, who tells him indifferently that he had given up his ideas of qualifying for a degree long ago. He has, in Jude's eyes and in his own as well, been a failure. Thus, Jude cannot see how he can succeed if his admired master, who, by the way, barely remembers him, having had thousands of students since, has failed in this way. Meeting Phillotson in these circumstances is very bad for Jude's morale. Meanwhile, Sue has broken with Miss Fontover, her landlady and one of her employers, and it turns out that the occasion for this was Miss Fontover's discovery of the statues of Venus and Apollo, which she had smashed, though they belonged to Sue. But Miss Fontover thought they smacked of paganism. Jude suggests to Sue that she resume teaching-in fact, Jude recommends her to Phillotson as an assistant teacher, to replace his former assistant. This comes about, though Jude's motive is not to help Phillotson, for whom he has lost respect, but to keep Sue near him, whether he quite admits this to himself or not.

Comment

The members of one of the marriage triangles of the novel meet in this chapter: Jude, Sue, and Phillotson. The symbolic meeting of Jude and Sue is "close to the cross ... which marked the spot Of the martyrdoms." This spot refers historically to that place in Oxford where, during certain religious persecutions, of the sixteenth century, several distinguished English clergymen and a number of laymen were burnt at the stake for holding heretical opinions on such theological questions as transubstantiation. But here, in the nineteenth century, Hardy implies, certain people are suffering another sort of persecution and martyrdom: a martyrdom resulting from outmoded concepts of marriage, religion, and education. Jude and Sue are to be the martyrs. This is the symbolic use Hardy makes of the place of their first meeting. Another ironic touch in this chapter occurs as we see that Jude was the person who brought about Sue's working for Phillotson as his assistant. Later Jude will come to regret this step he has taken regarding Sue.

Part Second: Chapter Five

Sue is now Phillotson's apprentice teacher. She is quite good at her work, and Phillotson wishes to keep her services. Everything in the secondary educational system is governed by Her Majesty's Education Code (H.M Education Code, to which Hardy refers). Though the code discourages such a relationship in various ways, and though Phillotson is old enough to be Sue's father, he becomes interested in Sue as a woman.

One day Sue and Phillotson take the school children to a pious exhibit: a model of the ancient city of Jerusalem. Sue is skeptical about the construction of the model, but this is nothing new; we have found her, in the course of the novel so far, to be skeptical and to doubt most generally-accepted things as not sufficiently verified to suit her. As she criticizes even the religious heritage of Jerusalem about which she says there was "nothing first-rate," suddenly she sees Jude at the exhibit. Phillotson tells Jude of Sue's critical outlook. She hastens to tell them both that she hates to be "what is called a clever girl." The truth is that she doesn't know what she is criticizing: She is really criticizing what she believes to be the unsatisfactory conditions of their present society and their present life.

Sue draws a perspective of the city, Jerusalem, in chalk on the blackboard for her students the following day, and shows that she remembers most of the details, better even that the teacher Phillotson can. On that day, the government school-inspector pays an unannounced visit to the school to see how well the teacher and his assistant are performing-as required by the law. Sue is upset, being inexperienced at such visits. But Phillotson has the instinct to protect her, and he tells her what is undoubtedly true: that she is the best teacher he ever had in the school or anywhere else.

Jude, meanwhile, looks forward impatiently to his next meeting with his cousin - but that Friday, he sees Phillotson "walking out" with Sue, or taking her out on a visit to the vicar. He is stricken with jealousy, and at the same time tells himself that Phillotson is too old for Sue. But, as Hardy says, "he could not interfere." Was he not Arabella's? Legally, he is still Arabella's husband, and could not afford a divorce from her even if he could get one. To marry Sue would be a criminal as well as a moral offense. While Phillotson is perhaps twenty and more years older than Sue, yet he may turn out well as a husband for her. As this short chapter ends, Jude ironically tells himself that "the intimacy between his cousin and the schoolmaster had been brought about entirely by himself."

Comment

In this chapter, Jude falls more deeply in love with Sue. At the same time, Sue and Phillotson somehow become aware of their feeling for one another, and Phillotson decides that he wants to marry his young assistant. Jude is smitten with jealousy, and the reader can infer that there is a romantic triangle here and that some form of conflict and trouble for at least one of the parties is certain to result.

Part Second: Chapter Six

Even as Jude experiences the beginning of disaster in his relationship with Sue, he temporarily leaves Christminster for a return visit to Marygreen, where his aunt Drusilla, now of an advanced age, is ill. Despite himself, when he sees his aunt, he refers to Sue. She is immediately on her guard, because as we have seen previously, Drusilla was strongly opposed even to his meeting or corresponding with Sue, as though she had a premonition of what would happen. "Don't you be a fool about her!" says his aunt. "She's a pert little thing... with her tight, strained nerves." His aunt reminds him that his marrying Arabella was the very worst, most self-destructive thing he could possibly have done, but if he gets involved with Sue, what is likely to happen will be even worse.

Again using the dramatic method, Hardy employs a minor character, the nurse of aunt Drusilla, who is also an elderly woman of the vicinity, to reveal more of Sue's character. She tells Jude some additional things about Sue that he hadn't known - this is gradual revelation of character not by auctorial **exposition** or direct comment, but by the comments of another character. Sue had been in her girlhood very artistic, literary, and dramatic-she was somewhat of an actress, as we have already realized. Both she and Jude had "seemed to see things in the air." She evidenced a man's mind, at least to the older women of the village such as Drusilla and her nurse.

After the discussion about Sue, Jude goes dressed in his best clothes, for it is Sunday, and meets other townspeople. They ask him about Christminster. Has he succeeded in entering a college? they want to know. Jude answers by saying that Christminster is all that he had hoped it would be, and more-it is "a unique center of thought and religion - the intellectual and spiritual granary of this country." What he does not add is that he is beginning to realize, at least subconsciously, that if it is a granary, it is an empty granary for him. He does not have enough money, he tells his listeners frankly, to get into a college. Since he must work full-time, he has not been able to improve his Greek sufficiently to take the entrance examinations. Looking more closely into his own situation, Jude sees that he has been stumbling in the dark with his private study.

Upon his return to Christminster, therefore, and after carefully studying a number of men who are the heads of important colleges, Jude writes letters to five heads of colleges, outlining his situation and requesting their advice. Meanwhile, as he awaits the replies of these gentlemen, Jude makes further inquiries and finds that without skilled coaching and instruction it would be almost impossible for a student to learn enough to qualify for one of the open (that is, open to any competitor) scholarships or "exhibitions" (an exhibition being generally a free grant to a worthy student to enable him to continue his education-like a scholarship or fellowship), though theoretically the winning of such an award is not completely outside the realm of possibility, provided that the student is quite brilliant. But Jude is not an extremely brilliant young man, although he is bright. Hardy makes this clear for his own purposes; the meaning of the book, it goes without saying, would have been quite different had Jude been successful in entering a college. But as we will see in this chapter, he hasn't much of a chance.

The only other way for him to enter a college is to "buy himself in." It would take him fifteen years at his present rate of earning as a workman to accumulate sufficient money to have some chance of paying the college fees. Jude sees, as he figures all this out, that he has been naive. "The whole scheme had burst up, like an iridescent soap-bubble, under the touch of a reasoned inquiry." That afternoon, which he is always to remember, he awakens from his nearly life-long dream. Looking into the heart of reality, he sees that his efforts, carried on over at least ten years, have been fruitless. This in turn brings Jude even closer to the thought of Sue. His destiny lies, not among the scholars, but among the workers and the ordinary people of the world, "the obscure." Just as he begins thinking this way, a letter arrives for him from the head of one of the colleges:

"Biblioll College

"Sir, - I have read your letter with interest; and, judging from your description of yourself as a workingman, I venture to think that you will have a much better chance of success in life by remaining in your own sphere and sticking to your trade than by adopting any other course. That, therefore, is what I advise you to do.

Yours faithfully, T. Tetuphenay.

"To Mr. J. Fawley, Stone-cutter."

This curt note signalizes the end of Jude's dreams and hopes. As no man can live without hope, Jude's mind will inevitably be turned to another object. Jude walks out into The Fourways, in the middle of the city, and thinks of the thousands and thousands of unknown people who had passed through that place, during hundreds of years extending back into dim antiquity. "The town life was a book of humanity infinitely more palpitating, varied, and compendious than the gown life." Or so Jude thinks now. Going to a public hall, he participates in the entertainment there of the townspeople, does some drinking though he does not become really drunk, and about ten o'clock walks back to his rooms, by way of the gate of the college the master of which had just so rudely written to him, the fictitious "Biblioll College." Jude pauses by the gate, and writes the following on the wall with a piece of chalk that as a stone-cutter he always carries:

"I have understanding as well as you; I am not inferior to you: yea, who knoweth not such things as these?" - Job xii.3.

This is a cry of despair; it could be Jude's epitaph.

Comment

The action of this important chapter largely speaks for itself. It is probably the most crucial chapter within the first two parts of *Jude the Obscure*, as well as being one of the longest. Jude is here overtaken by another personal disaster, but one of greater magnitude than had been the case when he so unwisely married Arabella. For that had been a young man's honest, if unwise, mistake. But this event in Christminster strikes Jude very deeply and wounds him. He sees that what he has worked for through many years was an illusion and was really beyond him all the time, not necessarily because of his lack of ability. He has the ability to be a scholar, given other circumstances of environment. But he is not by any means a genius to whom all things come naturally and easily. Hardy implies that the social and educational structures are such that a man like Jude, of whom there are thousands-above average, bright, clever, but not supremely brilliant-cannot overcome them. What Jude really suffers here is the loss of hope, and because of this he is in a most perilous state at the end of this chapter.

Part Second: Chapter Seven

Jude has fallen into a state of profound depression; "deprived of the objects of both intellect and emotion, he could not proceed to his work." He is especially depressed because he knows that he may not marry Sue because of his previous marriage to Arabella. Unable to bear the gloomy atmosphere of his room, he goes for distraction to an obscure tavern. Spending the day there, when he should have been at his work, he wallows in self-contempt. Later in the day several workmen, including some in his own trade, arrive and order a round of drinks while they gossip about the inner workings of Christminster society. Jude by this time is somewhat drunk, and he addresses the company about scholarship and learning. Several college undergraduates, as well as two women of questionable virtue, join the group. Jude speaks of his ill-treatment at not being given the chance to prove himself as a scholar.

The tavern audience insists that Jude offer his proofs on the spot: "Canst say the Creed in Latin, man?" asks Uncle Joe, one of the stone-masons. Of course he will - and Jude, downing a small Scotch, begins: "Credo in unum Deum, Patrem Omnipotentem ..." An undergraduate, sitting in the tavern, praises the Latin, while having "not the slightest conception of a single word" except the last one: Amen. Finally Jude, coming to himself a bit, calls them all arrogantly a "pack of fools" and leaves the tavern in disgust, more for himself than for his companions.

Not wishing to return to his lodgings, Jude decides to go to Sue. He appears at her cottage and abjectly confesses all he has done to himself and to his reputation. He feels himself to be very wicked indeed-all he has actually done is gotten drunk and spoken, "talked big," in a tavern. He finds Sue to be sympathetic, as he knew she would be, and she allows him to sleep downstairs in the house. In the morning he awakes, and overcome with remorse at his behavior of the day before, he leaves the house early as he is unwilling to face Sue. He decides to go back to Marygreen, having been dismissed from his job in the stone-yard, apparently for excessive absence. Having no money in his pockets, he walks, and this gives him a chance to sober up as the distance is twenty miles. In his own eyes, he is falling deeper into the abyss: the "hell of conscious failure."

Coming finally to Aunt Drusilla's cottage in Marygreen, Jude, by now at least outwardly recovered, meets the young curate, Mr.

Highridge, who has been comforting his aunt in her illness. Jude discusses his problems with him: he sees himself as "a fellow gone to the bad, though I had the best intentions in the world at one time." Possibly this is Hardy's ironic reference to the saying: "The road to hell is paved with good intentions." At any rate, Jude explains his plans and hopes, and Mr. Highridge is interested in him. He says that if Jude feels a real call to the ministry, he ought to consider entering the Church as a licentiate, which would not require graduation from a university. Jude finds this idea attractive, and determines to go through with this plan, as this first of the two parts of the novel set in Christminster comes to its end.

Comment

This chapter is in the nature of a descent into the underworld for Jude, or his being portrayed as the Prodigal Son who wastes his time and substance before returning abjectly to his home. There are, at any rate, Biblical overtones in it. Jude specifically describes himself as being in hell, though this may be the liquor talking and not Jude. If by hell is meant, whether in religious or non-religious terms, a state characterized by the absence of hope, Jude is indeed in hell - though a glimmering of hope is offered to him right at the end of this part.

Part Second, then, has structural and thematic affinities with Part First. In both, Jude begins hopefully and ends badly, at least in his own eyes, and in the eyes of the Marygreen villagers who are both his neighbors and a sort of Greek chorus, observing and commenting on his actions. But in Part Second, the degree of his fall is the greater. His marriage to Arabella in Part First is a disaster, but it does not rob him of hope, whereas his failure to make any headway at all in Christminster, the city of his lifelong dreams and ambitions, at least for the time being deprives him of any wish to continue striving. Added to this is the hopelessness of his attraction to Sue. They cannot marry, not only because they are cousins, but because of Jude's previous marriage. They would be bigamists, which then as now is a criminal offense, as well as a transgression of religious law. And thus, by the end of Part Second, all of Jude's bright hopes and plans have fallen apart, and he is crushed by life. But he is still young, and the human spirit has reserves of strength and resilience with which to resist. Meanwhile, there is the offered hope of a career of self-sacrifice in the Church, and to this Jude now hopes to address himself. But it may be that fate has other plans for him.

JUDE THE OBSCURE

TEXTUAL ANALYSIS

PART THIRD

Part Third ("At Melchester"): Chapter One

Having undergone the two progressively worse disasters in Parts One and Two respectively, Jude now at least temporarily abandons the world and determines to lead a religious life of faith and good works, "the ecclesiastical and altruistic life, as distinct from the intellectual and emulative life." Jude has the self-knowledge to see that his dreams of becoming a bishop through the Church and the university route which he had mapped out had as much of self-interest as love of his fellow human beings. Therefore, he thinks that if he were to enter the Church as a licentiate, as the curate had suggested, this would guarantee a purely altruistic motivation, for he would have scarcely any chance of ever rising higher than the rank of a humble curate, ministering to an obscure village or a city slum. This would be his particular self-chosen purgatory in his own view, not that the doctrine of the Church which he wishes to serve embraces a purgatorial state. Jude feels that he owes some recompense to God for what he considers his previous dissolute life. In this he is naive, for he has been more sinned against than sinning.

Meanwhile, he is considered a failure by the villagers of Marygreen. The situation is simple in their eyes: he has gone away to try to better himself, but has come back, and simply his presence speaks louder for the fact of his failure than anything he can say. The people evaluate him at less than his true worth as a person. But then, the world intrudes in the form of a letter from Sue, who tells Jude that as she has won a scholarship from the government, she is going to study at a training college at Melchester. (Melchester is identifiable as the English town of Salisbury, which has a notable cathedral.) Melchester also has a theological college, and Jude becomes interested from a professional point of view (he tells himself) to go to Melchester following Sue's footsteps, where he could study Divinity in preparation for his entering the Church as a licentiate. It is not Christminster, but it is something, and Jude has the thought that he could begin his ministry if he can graduate from the theological college at the age of thirty, the age at which Christ traditionally began His public life and teaching.

Jude continues his work back at Marygreen, mainly doing stone-cutting and lettering on headstones and monuments. After Christmas, with Sue studying at the training college at Melchester and apparently established and happy there, Jude receives a sudden letter from Sue in which she sounds quite miserable in her loneliness. She asks Jude to come, saying that she now wishes that she had never listened to Richard Phillotson, for he was the one who had advised her to come to Melchester and study for her certificate as a teacher. Phillotson of course also desires to marry Sue, and Jude sees that somehow her unhappiness must be tied up with her relations to Phillotson.

He decides to go at once, packing up his belongings and moving to Melchester. Upon his arrival, he visits the famous cathedral, and observes that much restorative stone-work will be needed in the interior and indeed is being done, which will assure his employment, for his skills in this line are in demand.

Meeting Sue, Jude apologizes for his conduct when they had last seen each other in Christminster, and they walk out together. What Sue hates about the college she is in is the restraint. She is not used to such confinement. Jude impulsively tells her his belief that Phillotson actually wanted to marry her - "an old man like him!" After first denying any interest on Phillotson's part, she suddenly reverses her story and says that Phillotson has asked her to marry him after she completes the two-year training college course, and further, that she has agreed to do so. Their plan after marriage is for them to take charge of a large coeducational school in which Phillotson will manage the classes of boys and Sue the classes of girls. For Jude, Sue "was something of a riddle to him." She is a riddle wrapped in an enigma, but quite believable in her emotionalism and confusion. While they part, Jude thinks more and more of her, and meanwhile he works into some very good employment in the restoration work on the cathedral. He takes lodgings near the Close gate - that is near the boundaries of the ground belonging to the cathedral and its attached quarters. And to further his studies he acquires a library of theological works: the Church Fathers, Paley, Butler, Newman, and Pusey. With this he seems to have found some satisfaction in his life.

Comment

In this chapter, Jude seems to have recovered from his previous difficulties, and to be leading a sober and well-regulated life of work and study, with his emotional satisfactions obtained from his curious relationship with Sue. At this point it is Sue's character which is baffling, not Jude's. Jude seems to have almost everything that he wants, except Christminster, and to be living in a state of relative contentment compared to what he had previously been through with Arabella, in his early childhood, and in the shattering of his dreams of a university career at Christminster.

Part Third: Chapter Two

One afternoon Sue, having a half-day's leave from her strictly supervised college surroundings, goes with Jude on a visit to Wardour Castle near Melchester. They go by train. Upon arrival at the castle, Jude spends his time looking at the religious and devotional pictures in the art gallery, by del Sarto and others. Sue is not as interested in religious art. When they finish their tour of the castle, they decide, perhaps from a sense of the freedom they have found that afternoon, to walk seven miles to another train station in order to catch the return train to Melchester. The walk takes them longer than they had imagined it would; Sue especially is quite tired. As they stop to rest at a small cottage adjoining a sheepfold, the shepherd there tells them that they have miscalculated: the train will be gone no matter how fast they run. He offers them accommodation for the night at the cottage. They tell him that they are not married, and arrange to have separate rooms. The shepherd wakes them up the next morning very early, and they catch the next train to Melchester. Sue expresses a certain apprehension about her reception at the training college since she had been away without permission - and she observes the questioning glance on the face of the doorkeeper, or porter, as Jude brings her to the door of the college and there leaves her.

Comment

Again in this chapter we observe the use Hardy makes of coincidence or accident to determine a character's ultimate destiny. This apparently trivial event: the missing of the train and the taking of the next one in the morning, though entirely innocent on the parts of Jude and Sue, is to have momentous consequences for Sue, and through her, for Jude.

Though Sue and Jude are, it bears repeating, innocent of any wrongdoing here, perhaps, as they were happy in each other's company, they subconsciously delayed their return. But this is hardly a shortcoming which calls for the kind of punishment Sue is to experience as a result of this absence.

Part Third: Chapter Three

Hardy calls the training college "a species of nunnery." It is an establishment attended by about seventy young women, of whom Sue is one-most of them around the age of twenty or twenty-one. They are under rigid supervision. Upon it being rumored that Sue had not come in that night, several of the girls nod knowingly: "She went out with her young man." Although she had said that he was her cousin, this is not believed and nobody thinks to check the truth of her statement. In the evening, when the roll is called and communal prayers and hymns are offered, all the girls wonder where Sue is. Her cot remains empty all night. In the morning, rumors abound as all see that she still has not returned, and very shortly the order comes down from the principal that when Sue returns, nobody is to speak to her without permission.

When Sue returns in the morning, she is immediately called to the principal's office, ordered to a solitary room for a week, also to take her meals there as punishment. She is severely reprimanded. The girls think this is too severe a punishment for Sue, and ask by petition that it be lessened, but the authorities pay no attention to the petition. Therefore, the students refuse to do their lessons and go on strike, all because of Sue. Meanwhile, the administration makes it known that Jude is not Sue's cousin, according to information it has claimed to receive from Christminster, to which they had written to find that Jude had been discharged from his work there for drunkenness and "blasphemy." Towards the end of that same day, it becomes known that Sue had gotten out the back window of the room in which she was confined, and had disappeared. They look everywhere, but cannot find her. The directress of the college is horrified, not so much because it is feared that Sue may have drowned in the river adjoining the buildings, but also because she fears a possible scandal. Upon investigation by lantern light, the authorities find footprints in one of the banks of the river - the opposite bank from the college, and this shows that at least Sue has not drowned.

That evening, while at his studies Jude hears some gravel thrown against his window pane. He finds that the person attracting his attention is Sue. She comes up to his room and warms herself by the fire, telling him meanwhile how unjustly she had been treated at the college. Jude gets dry clothes for her, leaving the room so that she can change. He also gets her a little brandy, being quite afraid that she has caught a chill from the water during her escape. Soon she is fast asleep. Jude spends the time simply admiring her; he saw in her "almost a divinity."

Comment

Chapter Three shows Sue being unjustly punished because the authorities at the college are more inclined to accept first appearances than to make any serious inquiry about her conduct. Sue is innocent, but is punished anyway, perhaps to set an example, and also because those who run the college fear that the good name of the institution may be clouded by scandal. This strict supervision, in Sue's case, only has the opposite effect of driving the unpredictable Sue-predictable, that is, only in her unpredictability-to escape. Thus ultimately the unjust actions of the authorities of the college bring about that which they had feared, for Sue runs away.

Hardy makes it clear that the concern which the college feels about Sue is hardly motivated by genuine worry about her well-being; instead, it is worry over the college's reputation. Indeed, all through this book, there is very little humanity displayed by people to each other, except, for some part of the work, between Sue and Jude. The typical relationship between human beings is, as Hardy portrays and interprets it, that between Arabella and Jude, or between the college and Sue, and in each case the former treats the latter as an object, not as a person.

Part Third: Chapter Four

At this point, Jude's landlady knocks on his door. Jude quickly hides Sue's clothes, and the landlady, seeing Sue, assumes that she is a young man visiting Jude. He orders supper in his rooms for both of them-perfectly proper, and the landlady thinks no more of the matter at this time. "I ought not to be here, ought I?"

observes Sue, because the hour is past ten in the evening. She knows that the authorities at the college will be furious with her. She remains, and she and Jude speak about philosophical negation and other abstract matters. She tells Jude what her reading and education have been: Defoe, Smollett, Fielding, Shakespeare, the Bible-not the theological and Greek and Latin originals which Jude has been reading. In fact, she has read more than Jude, and it is reading that a girl of her age, in Victorian England, would not generally have done. A "proper" education for her might have been sewing, knitting, music, drawing - but not serious literature and philosophy.

She confides in Jude that she never has had any fear of men; she has mixed with them "almost as one of their own sex." This is a significant statement for the further establishment of her character. She further confides in Jude that when she was eighteen she became intimate, but not in the usual sense of the term as involving the sexual relationship, with an undergraduate at Christminster; this explains a good deal of her reading, because the student had helped her in her education. After taking his degree at his college, the student had asked Sue to become his mistress, but she had refused him. Both, however, went to London, where he became a leader-writer for a great London daily newspaper. And, most strangely, they shared a sitting-room for fifteen months without Sue giving in and becoming his mistress, though they lived together. This curious relationship apparently broke the young man's heart, and he came home from a trip abroad only to die. He left Sue a little money, "probably because she had broken his heart," Hardy observed.

This bizarre story she tells with a significant lack of emotionalism. The Christminster student "could never have believed" of any woman that she could have held out against him for such a long time. For her, as she tells Jude, what the story proves is that "men are so much better than women." But it also proves something about her: that she is even more of a destructive force in her relationships with men than is Arabella, who is so frankly sensual and selfish. What money Sue received from the estate of her "friend" was lost in a bubble scheme - that is, a highly speculative investment which collapsed suddenly. Sue's father had refused to take her back, as she had disgraced the family in his eyes. Jude tells Sue that he believes her to be both innocent and unconventional. "People say," she tells him, "that I must be cold-natured-sexless." She also adds that she had told Phillotson about the relationship with the Christminster student.

Jude feels very depressed at hearing the story, probably because it shows him an aspect of Sue that he had not observed before and which he realizes is very destructive. Changing the subject, he invites Sue to join him at his evening prayers, for he has not only been reading theology lately, he has also been attempting to live his religious beliefs. Sue says that she would prefer not to join him in these exercises, and speaks bitterly against Christminster and the religious views for which it stands. Her friend, the student, had been "the most irreligious man I ever knew, and the most moral." We do not exactly see the evidence for this, from what she herself has said. Sue touches Jude painfully as she tells him, truly: "You are one of the very men Christminster was intended for when the Colleges were founded - a man with a passion for learning, but no money, or opportunity, or friends, who are elbowed off the pavement by the millionaires' son." She is really bitter at the university.

Jude then turns the conversation to Phillotson, but he notices that though Sue is both Phillotson's protegee and his betrothed, she is very reluctant to speak of him. She offers to write for Jude a "new" New Testament, by cutting up the Gospels and rearranging them in chronological order as written: this is a reflection of the Higher Criticism of the Bible, which, originating earlier in the nineteenth century in Germany, regarded the Bible as a historical text subject to evaluation and not a work solely of Divine inspiration. In this, too, Sue shows herself one of the "advanced" members of Victorian society. She launches, improbably, into an attack on the usual method of interpreting the Song of Solomon: that it is an allegorical song of Christ to His mystical bride, the Church. She says that the Song of Solomon is to be taken literally, as a great celebration of human love, not of the Divine. And she criticizes Jude, saying that she had hopes that he would be her "comrade," but apparently he is too steeped in tradition and superstition.

Jude has not mentioned the existence of Arabella to her up to this point. He continues to keep silent on this matter, and they fall asleep, or she does, sitting in her chair, while Jude admires her as though she is Ganymede, a young boy beloved of the gods in Greek mythology, sometimes portrayed in the myth as the cupbearer to the gods. But the cup she will bring to Jude will be a bitter one; she will bring no liberating wine to him.

Comment

This is one of the most curious chapters in the entire novel, and one of the most important, for in the dialogue between Sue and Jude, Hardy takes an opportunity to inject criticisms of all three Victorian institutions which he has chosen to satirize and pillory in this novel: Marriage, the Church, and the Universities.

We discover, from Sue's behavior to Jude, and even more to the young Christminster student, that she is very destructive in her relationships with men, whether she is conscious of it or not. She apparently has no understanding of what her behavior did and is doing to Jude. D.H. Lawrence wrote a very provocative essay about the character of Sue Bridehead, as one might have expected of him. (See Bibliography.)

A reader familiar with Lawrence's own fiction can predict the strong reaction he would have against Sue's character.

The main function of this chapter, then, is to focus and draw together the three main objects of Hardy's **satire**, and also, further to establish Sue's character.

Part Third: Chapter Five

In the morning, Sue dresses in her own clothes, now dry, and leaves the house quietly with Jude, without being observed, they both suppose. She plans to return to the training college and be readmitted. They part at the railroad station, and her last words to Jude are "you mustn't love me." Jude is to "like" her only. He next receives a sort of letter of apology from her the next morning. "If you want to love me," she says, "you may." The next Sunday Jude visits her to find her in bed; the training college had refused to have her back, and the authorities had further suggested that she marry Jude as quickly as possible for the sake of her reputation. Jude cannot marry her or anyone else, as he is already married, although Arabella is, as far as he is aware, in Australia. Jude and Sue have another unsatisfactory meeting, and Jude leaves her, but promptly there comes another note from her: she is coming to Melchester the next Saturday to get her belongings from the training college, and she would like to walk with him for a bit. He is agreeable to this.

Comment

This chapter further intensifies the impression that Sue, though an attractive girl, does not understand the devastating damage that she wreaks on men by her impulsiveness-especially on Jude. The reader of *Jude the Obscure* comes to realize at this point that Sue is a more destructive force, as far as Jude is concerned, than the frankly selfish and animalistic Arabella had ever been.

Part Third: Chapter Six

At the beginning of Chapter Six, the schoolmaster Phillotson has moved from the vicinity of Christminster, where he and Jude had become reacquainted after a lapse of so many years, to Shaston, his native town about sixty miles south of Christminster. He is directing a large boys' school, and is saving money and decorating his new house in expectation of his marriage to Sue Phillotson, who is something of an antiquarian-Hardy uses this character trait in him for symbolic purposes-studies Britannic antiquities. His essential lack of vitality is what Hardy seems to wish to bring out by assigning him these interests. Even his physical description gives the impression of antiquity and obscure lack of well-being; his face is "unhealthy-looking," and an "old-fashioned" face. Thinking of Sue, Phillotson decides to pay an unannounced visit to the training college, and though Sue had been expelled there two weeks earlier, she had not written to Phillotson telling him what had happened. Phillotson is quite taken aback at the news that Sue is no longer a student at the college, especially when he hears the reason the authorities give: that she had behaved in a suspicious and compromising manner with a young man and had absented herself overnight from the college without leave. Phillotson, reflecting of this news, enters the adjacent cathedral for a moment, and there he sees Jude, one of the workmen repairing the interior stone-work.

Jude and Phillotson had not seen much of each other for some time; Phillotson possibly seeing in Jude a potential, if not actual, rival for Sue's affections, and Jude not only seeing Phillotson as his rival in love, but also regarding him as the embodiment of failure-of his, Jude's, failed aspirations. For Phillotson had been no more successful than Jude in winning admission to Christminster and taking a degree. He had given up the idea years earlier. The two men speak about Sue, and Jude is in a perfect position to tell Phillotson a lying tale - that the authorities had been well-advised to expel Sue, and that she was no longer as innocent as Phillotson had supposed. The lie would have ensured that Phillotson would have lost interest in Sue, and Jude could have had her for himself. So Hardy implies. Jude is, in the serious things of life, quite honest, and here will not stoop to slander Sue, defying the maxim that "all's fair in love and war." Most honorably he reassures Phillotson of the truth of Sue's innocence. He tells Phillotson that he, Jude, would like to marry Sue but he cannot. Jude swears that the suspicion which led to Sue's rustication (rustication being an English term for expulsion, temporary or permanent, from a school or college) is an absolutely baseless one. "So help me God!" Jude adds. Phillotson believes him.

Afterwards, Jude meets Sue as she has returned to get her possessions from the college, and tells her of his marriage to Arabella. She feels that Jude was cruel in not telling her of this earlier; she seems quite unreasoningly jealous, in view of her erratic treatment of Jude when she knew nothing of his previous marriage. She asks Jude if Arabella is a pretty woman, "even if she is wicked." Jude is bitter, seeing the consequences of his unwise marriage to Arabella continuing. He cannot marry Sue.

Meanwhile, Sue speaks against the authorities of the training college; their views "of the relations of man and woman are limited as is proved by their expelling me from the school," and she adds: "their philosophy only recognizes relations based on animal desire." Jude tells her what his aunt Drusilla had told him as a young boy: the Fawleys were not meant for marriage. She makes light of this prophecy. For her, the Fawleys may have been unlucky in their choice of marriage partners, but nothing further is signified by the family's past. As the chapter ends, they agree that they can continue to be friends, but nothing more.

Comment

Here a bit more of Hardy's essential criticism of the narrowness of Victorian England, with its strict interpretation of the marriage relationship, is further manifested, in the character of Phillotson primarily and Sue secondarily. It will be significant in the later action of the novel that Phillotson does listen to Jude as he describes the circumstances of Sue's expulsion from the college. A more trusting and honorable man would, Hardy implies, have refused to listen to any of these stories about the character of his prospective wife, trusting her implicitly as he had chosen her freely.

Part Third: Chapter Seven

A formal note from Sue, signed with her full name: Susanna Florence Mary Bridehead, arrives in Jude's hands a couple of days after the preceding events; it announces that Sue and Phillotson are to be married in three or four weeks. Jude "staggered under the news" - but what can he do about it? He suspects that the news of his own marriage to Arabella may have triggered her impulsive decision. Sue then writes, asking Jude as her "only married relation" to give her away at the wedding. Jude answers at once, generously agreeing to give her away and suggesting that it would be proper for her to be married from his house. Upon her accepting this offer, Jude moves in to larger quarters, and presently Sue comes into residence in the same house, but on a different floor, for the required ten days so that she will establish residence in the appropriate parish prior to her marriage. She is planning to be married in a church: the church of St. Thomas. She does not believe in the rituals of the church, or in its laws regarding marriage - in fact, Jude thinks: "she does not even know what marriage means!" Apparently he is right. He thinks further that the reason she wants the ceremonial trappings of the marriage, in which she does not believe, is that she is "an epicure in emotions." She enjoys emotional situations, but we are a little in the dark as to her actual motive in marrying Phillotson, a man old enough to be her father. Perhaps the relatively simple explanation that she is marrying him "on the rebound" from Jude, as Jude himself suspects, is the most logical one, not that we are to expect logic from Sue Bridehead. She really seems such a contradiction: so innocent and naive about marriage, and yet so sophisticated and "advanced" in her views about the institution, that whatever we think of her views, we may predict that she is in for something of a rude awakening. For while the intellectual side of her nature is well developed - Jude calls her a "female Shelley" at one point, and this is by way of compliment, for the poet Shelley was of enormous intellectual power, still the emotional side of Sue is that of a child, at least at the time of her marriage to Phillotson.

Phillotson arrives, and all prepare for the marriage ceremony. In due course they go to the church. Jude thinks, as the ceremony is being performed, that Sue is somehow perversely cruel and unfeeling, to ask him to do such a thing as give her away at her marriage, knowing as she does how he feels about her. He is more than ever convinced that she does not know what the marriage relationship is, and that she is making a ghastly mistake by marrying Phillotson. Was this retaliation against him? Jude asks himself. As Sue leaves the church with Phillotson, she seems about to say something serious to Jude, but thinks better of it, so that whatever she had meant to say remains unspoken.

Comment

This chapter reveals additional facets of Sue Bridehead's character: that she is a woman who, quite unconsciously, is immensely destructive to men, and that in getting married to Phillotson she doesn't know what she is doing. Jude realizes this, but still cannot free himself from his attraction to her.

Part Third: Chapter Eight

Melchester is no longer a place where Jude can stay, for it has too many unhappy associations for him. He wonders if Sue on her wedding day meant to confess to him that she loved him and not Phillotson. An inner voice tells him that she will leave Phillotson now and not go home with him - that she will change her mind. It is a wild hope, and he meditates on "the scorn of Nature for man's finer emotions," which is one of Hardy's major theses in this problem-novel. But at any rate Sue does not return, and Jude's hope is a fantasy.

Very soon after the wedding, Jude receives news that his aunt Drusilla is seriously ill. At the same time, he receives a letter from his old employer at Christminster offering him a good job if he will return there. So Jude decides to see his aunt first and then to go on to Christminster. When he comes back to Marygreen, he finds Drusilla near death, although the Widow Edlin, who has been caring for her, tells him that she may linger on for weeks. Jude writes at once to Sue, suggesting that she come-he writes with the intention of meeting Sue the next evening as he returns from Christminster. As he arrives in Christminster, Sue is now present in his consciousness as a phantom replacing the ancient scholars and churchmen, upon whom Jude had focused his attention earlier.

Jude finds himself unwilling to return to work in the stone-cutting yard; it is too depressing to him in view of the associations Christminster has for him. So he goes to a public-house to have a drink. In the bar, where he has gone with an old acquaintance he has met on the street, Tinker Taylor, he sees two barmaids. To his amazement, one of them is Arabella. He is further astounded to hear Arabella tell a Christminster undergraduate, one Mr. Cockman, that she had left her husband "in Australia." Jude hears the lie, and even as he does so, Arabella sees and recognizes Jude. She is properly startled, but recovers quickly as she always does. Then she speaks to him with a humorous impudence in her eye - "I thought you were underground years ago!" Arabella, it turns out, had returned from Sydney three months previously. She questions Jude about what had become of him after they parted, and he answers: "I am as I was." Jude observes that Arabella is still wearing a wedding ring, with what is apparently a sapphire of some value, and that she is passing as married. Jude reflects that in the eyes of the Church he is married to Arabella, whatever his other interests may be at present. They arrange to meet that evening. He further reflects that perhaps Arabella's reappearance is an intended Divine intervention, to punish him for his unlawful love for Sue. He thinks of the appointment he has made to meet Sue that night, and knows that Sue will be disappointed when he does not appear at the railroad station. He knows that he should be back to see his aunt Drusilla. They take the evening train to Aldbrickham and engage a room while Arabella, who can get the following day off, offers to come back to Marygreen with him. Jude accepts, while sick and tired already of her and of himself.

Comment

Here, of course, is another fantastic coincidence of the kind which abounds in Hardy's novels. These coincidences have a fated inevitability: Jude meeting Arabella at this time, in this place, indicates the impossibility of his escaping his fate.

In the morning, Arabella has decided to go back to work in the bar at eleven o'clock. They have not agreed that she will come with Jude after all to see his aunt. As they walk in the direction of Alfredston, Jude sighs: "Ah, poor feeble me! This is the very road by which I came into Christminster years ago full of plans." Arabella says that she has something to tell Jude: that she has married again, and her second "husband" is a hotel-keeper in Australia, whom she has left behind. She does not seem to consider this bigamous marriage a crime, though she had a living husband, and she tells Jude so. The law and the Church both consider this an offense, if it were to be revealed, and so she asks Jude to say and do nothing about what she has done—relying on his good nature. He agrees. "Why didn't you tell me this last night?" demands Jude. She has no answer for him. They had been together as man and wife that night, and Jude would not have been a party to this relationship had he known of her other marriage.

Arabella has no sense of guilt; she says that many people "over there" have done just this. "How did I know where you were?" she says to him. There is one thing more she wants to tell him, even as he returns to Christminster, feeling a sense of degradation. He pities Arabella, even while he condemns her. Suddenly, at the railway station, Sue appears. She is glad to see Jude, and she tells him that having gone to Marygreen she had seen his aunt Drusilla, who was a bit better. Now Sue is returning. He contrasts Sue with Arabella, and Sue appears to him as a divinity, in comparison with the animalistic Arabella. Sue does not wish Jude to talk about her or about her marriage to Phillotson. At this point, he decides not to tell Sue about Arabella's return or about the fact that they had spent the night together at an inn. Jude is sure not so much from what Sue says about Phillotson, who is apparently a model husband, but from her expression and her nervousness, that while Sue had been married less than a month, she is already most unhappy. When Jude refers to her as Mrs. Phillotson, she reproaches him by a glance. In turn he points out, near Marygreen, the small cottage in which he and Arabella had lived, quarreled, and parted. Sue makes the remark: "That was to you, Jude, what the schoolhouse at Shaston is to me!" It is absolutely clear to Jude that somehow Sue feels that she should not have married Phillotson.

They arrive at aunt Drusilla's cottage, and to their surprise find the old lady up and about, in defiance of medical advice. "Ah, you'll rue this marrying as well as he!" she says to Sue. "All you family do." Drusilla says that Phillotson is perhaps a nice person, but she can't stand him and she can't see how any other woman could either. Sue is crying, and when Jude inquires why, she tells him that it is because what aunt Drusilla says is true. "I ought not to have married!" Jude tries to forget Sue as a woman again, staying at his aunt's cottage in Marygreen, where he reads Church history, the ascetics, and the Church Fathers. While he is there a letter posted in London arrives from Arabella, informing him that her husband-her bigamous second husband, who no doubt does not even know of Jude's existence, is coming to England to take a public-house in Lambeth. She has decided that she is more attracted towards the Australian man than towards Jude, and she bids Jude goodbye, telling him that she bears him no ill-will and hopes he will not turn against her. In this last comment is seen the full character of Arabella, who in her frank earthiness has sometimes seemed to readers almost admirable. She has just about ruined Jude, not once but several times - and here she tells him that she bears him no ill will!

Comment

In this chapter we have learned what Jude suspected all along: that Sue's marriage to Phillotson would turn out to be as much of a disaster to her as had been his marriage to Arabella. Both marriages had been hastily entered into, and for reasons that were not substantial. Thus, by the end of this chapter the two marital triangles are now fully established: Jude being the key to both. Arabella is married to two husbands simultaneously (of course her second marriage is legally null and void, and in Victorian England would probably have earned her a five-year term in prison had it been discovered) and she is relying on Jude's sense of honor not to denounce her. Sue, who is married to Richard Phillotson, but not happily, is again attracted to Jude, and Jude is still in love with her, in defiance of all **convention** and of his own religious training. So the chapter closes, with five tangled lives that give every promise of becoming even more tangled.

Part Third: Chapter Ten

The last chapter of Part Third seems to end with an anti-climax. There is no absolute disaster in Part Third, unless we can call

Arabella's return and Sue's marriage disasters-both of them being blows to Jude's emotional well-being. Jude returns to Melchester, because Shaston, where Sue is now living, is less than twenty miles away from Melchester. With the peculiar ascetic outlook that Jude has now, he feels the temptation to visit Sue will be a good thing for his spiritual health: he will win glory by resisting the temptation purely on a voluntary basis. Thus he deceives himself, rationalizing the perfectly understandable desire he has at least to live near Sue, though she is the wife of another. He hopes that he can acquire further self-discipline.

Jude returns somewhat feverishly to his studies for the Anglican priesthood, as something to cling to. He has overcome his tendency to resort to liquor, and despises himself for having been weak to the point that he had even temporarily gone back to his wife, Arabella. He is gaining at least the self-knowledge to see that he was "a man of too many passions to make a good clergyman; the utmost he could hope for was that in a life of constant internal warfare between flesh and spirit, the former might not always be victorious." Jude develops skill in Church music and singing, which of course are related to his studies in Divinity.

He joins a choir in a village church near Melchester, and about Easter he hears a new hymn during choir practice which particularly appeals to him; it is called "The Foot of the Cross." The hymn moves Jude exceedingly, and he asks the organist of the church who the composer is. It is a local man, he is told - a professional musician at Kennetbridge, near Christminster, who was brought up and educated in Christminster traditions. The hymn is being sung everywhere for Easter. Jude idealizes the unknown composer and on impulse decides to visit him. "He would understand my difficulties," Jude thinks, rather strangely. Jude finds out, "like the child that he was," the address of the man and determines to visit him the very next Sunday. He goes to Kennetbridge, is shown the composer's house, and introduces himself. "I must speak to that man!" Jude tells himself. Jude is admitted to the house. At first the composer is no doubt flattered to have such interest taken in his work by a stranger. But when Jude praises the hymn, he is appalled to hear the composer say of it: "Yet, I wrote it about a year ago ... there's money in it, if I could only see about getting it published. Music is a poor staff to lean on. I am giving it up entirely. There's no money in it. You must go into trade if you want to make money nowadays." He is thinking of going into the wine business, and hands Jude a list of wines that he is proposing to sell. Jude is taken quite by surprise, and is of course disappointed in his host. The composer, when he finds that Jude is a poor workman (from his speech and bearing, he had assumed Jude to be of higher social standing), changes his manner, becoming colder, and Jude takes the hint and leaves in embarrassment. He is very depressed at the unexpected outcome of this interview.

When Jude returns to Melchester by the slow Sunday train, he finds something that cheers him up even while disappointing him: an invitation from Sue to come that very day to have dinner with the Phillotson family. He has missed this opportunity because he received the letter only when too late to act upon it, so that the strange expedition to Kennetbridge seems to have been a Providential intervention to save him from temptation. At second thought, he finds himself beginning to doubt that God-or the gods-take special interest in sending such a person as himself on a fool's errand. Writing instantly to Sue in reply, he tells her of his regret at not responding quickly enough to her invitation - but he would like to come any convenient day in the week. Sue, after a delay, writes to him saying that she would like to have him visit them the Thursday before Good Friday. She is now assistant-teacher in her husband's school. Jude takes time off from his work on the cathedral restoration at Melchester for that day, and goes to Shaston.

Comment

This short chapter ends, if not in disaster, not in hope either, at least as Hardy presents Jude's situation to the reader. For Jude seems to be drifting as the prey of conflicting forces, and we feel that a resolution, a break of some sort which will probably injure Jude, will occur soon. His life cannot go on much longer in its current manner.

Part Third in its entirety sees Sue hastily and unwisely married to a man much older than herself - a man about whom she has the most ambiguous feelings. It sees Arabella's return from Australia, a self-confessed bigamist, and it sees Jude beginning to doubt his vocation in the Church. Though Hardy, subscribing to Victorian **convention**, does not say this in an overly direct manner, it is clear that Jude is torn by sexual passion which he somehow cannot fully acknowledge even to himself. But it would be a mistake to interpret this portion of the novel as simply an account of a young man's war against the temptations of the flesh, and his deceiving himself that his interest in Sue is what is inexactly called "Platonic." He wants her for his wife, and cannot have her because he is already married, as she is. Besides, there is a legitimate question whether she is really fit for marriage with anyone. The Fawley curse seems to operate even more in Sue's case than in Jude's.

JUDE THE OBSCURE

TEXTUAL ANALYSIS

PART FOURTH

Part Fourth ("At Shaston"): Chapter One

This part begins with an epigraph from Milton - a quotation from one of the tracts on divorce which the great poet wrote when he was examining (1643–45) the subject of marriage, in part because of his own marital unhappiness at the time. "Who so prefers either Matrimony or other Ordinance before the Good of Man and the plain Exigence of Charity, let him profess Papist, or Protestant, or what he will, he is no better than a Pharisee." This is a liberal interpretation of the marriage tie, implying that for good cause it may and indeed should be dissolved-whereas the Anglican Church of Hardy's day as well as the present, like the Roman Catholic, does not allow divorce, though for grave cause there may be separation. Ultimately this is derived from the text of the Gospels (Matthew 19: 6); the words of Christ to the Pharisees - "What therefore God hath joined together, let no man put asunder." But Hardy, like Milton in his tracts on divorce, only in a more extreme fashion, has a different view of the marriage relationship, and this view is present in *Jude the Obscure*.

This part takes place in Shaston, which is the old name of the famous town now known as Shaftesbury-also called in ancient times Palladour. It is one of the oldest towns continuously established in England, and King Alfred established here in 880 a convent for Benedictine nuns. Edward the Martyr, who died in 978, has his tomb here, according to tradition. And, more important for the symbolic use Hardy makes of the place, Shaston has many associations with the Church, dating back to the shrines nearly a thousand years old. In later days, Hardy observes ironically, Shaston fell from grace: "beer was more plentiful than water, and ... there were more wanton women than honest wives and maids."

Comment

By dwelling on the external physical and moral aspects of Shaston, past and present, Hardy without a doubt meant to symbolize what he considered to be the decadence of the formal religion of his age. Shaston, then, in the novel is not simply a city of churches and other ecclesiastical structures made of stone, which Jude spends a good part of his life repairing. It is the Church, at least as Hardy saw it: an institution with all the life gone.

Sue and Jude meet at the school operated by Phillotson and his helpmeet. Phillotson being at a meeting of teachers, Sue and Jude talk somewhat freely of their situations. Sue speaks of her "former friend," the now dead university student, whom she herself killed in a way. Suddenly the remembrance of this tragic and foolish young student, now several years dead, triggers a strong reaction in Jude. He speaks what is in his heart, for he has been stung into jealousy by Sue's mentioning the other young man. "Sue," he says unexpectedly, "I sometimes think you are a flirt." Sue is very upset at this, and invites Jude to leave at once. As he rises, she relents. Hinting that while she is called Mrs. Richard Phillotson, she is not so in her own mind, she invites Jude to come back the following week to visit her and Phillotson. And she implicitly apologizes for her "aberrant passions and unaccountable antipathies" - antipathies, we are led to see, which are directed not at Jude so much as at her husband, Phillotson. Jude knows at this point that as one who wishes to pursue the religious life he should break with Sue, but he feels sorry for her in what is evidently her miserable relationship with Phillotson. But in truth, whether he recognizes it or not, his human nature is more powerful in him by far than his spiritual nature. Yet at this point he still thinks of a career in the Church.

Comment

In chronicling the "deadly war between flesh and spirit" as embodied in *Jude the Obscure*, Hardy assigns little blame to Jude. He is presented, as in this chapter, as one who cannot help himself.

This is a simple way of saying that this novel, even more than Hardy's other works, contains elements of naturalism: the application of scientific determinism to fiction. For a further discussion of *Jude the Obscure* as a naturalistic novel, see the section in the survey of criticism on Jude below.

Part Fourth: Chapter Two

The chapter begins with a brief and rather cold four-line note from Susanna Florence Mary, cancelling the invitation to Jude to visit her the next week: "Don't come next week. On your own account don't. We were too free, under the influence of that morbid hymn and the twilight. Think no more than you can help of Susanna Florence Mary"

He answers briefly, agreeing with her. But he is bitterly disappointed. As they seem thus to have broken off with each other, finally, fate or coincidence steps in again. Jude receives a telegram from Marygreen. His aunt is dying, and he must come.

Only three-and-a-half hours later, when he arrives in Marygreen, he reads in the faces of the people that his aunt is dead. It was so, and he telegraphs to Sue telling her that the funeral will be that Friday. He doesn't know whether she will come, but at the last moment she appears by train, very nervous at meeting Jude. After the simple funeral ceremony, Sue and Jude return to Drusilla's cottage for tea, and discuss not the dead, but marriage. Sue asks Jude whether it would be possible for a wife to dislike her husband for no particular reason except a physical objection, a fastidiousness. Jude speculates that Sue is not happy in her marriage, and says this to her, but she insists that having been married eight weeks she is entirely happy. Nevertheless, Jude says that she oughtn't to have married Phillotson.

Jude further says that they can be cousins only-he feels nothing more for her, as Arabella has come back. This hit finally leads Sue to break down and admit what is already quite obvious to Jude: while she may admire Phillotson as a friend, he is torture as her husband. What horrifies and tortures her is, as she says, "the necessity of being responsive to this man whenever he wishes ... this dreadful contract to feel in a particular way in a matter whose essence is its voluntariness!" Again she indicts the institution of marriage, though it may be that she herself is really unfit for marriage.

That night, Jude cannot sleep, and he is awakened by the cry of a rabbit caught in a steel trap. He goes down and puts it out of its misery. Then Sue appears, from the Widow Edlin's house, having been awakened also by the sufferings of the trapped rabbit. She tells Jude something further about her relationship with Phillotson which he had suspected all along: she "had never thought out fully what marriage meant."

Comment

One of the symbols in this rather emotional chapter is the killing of the trapped rabbit; this is a characteristic symbolic sign used by Hardy, similar to the killing of the pig in Part First. The fates of the animals are equated with those of the human characters, who are equally trapped by fate or circumstance or coincidence or bad luck or the malevolence of whatever gods there be, in Hardy's view.

Part Fourth: Chapter Three

Early the next morning Sue and Jude set out for the railroad station again so that Sue can return to her husband. As they part and begin to go their separate ways, Sue and Jude suddenly return to each other and "embracing most unpremeditatedly, kissed close and long"; they seem drawn by forces stronger than they can resist. The kiss is a turning point in Jude's life. He decides, hours later as he thinks about the event, that he should not profess to be the servant of a religion "in which sexual love was regarded as at its best a frailty and at its worst damnation." He sees now that his aspirations have been checked by his attraction to women. Being consistent and still honest with himself, so far as he has insight into his own problems, he quietly performs a most radical action, considering his years of study: he digs a shallow hole in his garden, and placing therein all his theological books which represent his studies for months past, he burns them. Very systematically, he burns everything. At the end, he feels relief. Of course this action symbolizes his break with his aspirations for a religious life. Even as he does this, Sue, returning to her husband on the train, feels that she has done wrong, and betrayed her husband in spirit if not actually.

Comment

Hardy, in fairness to the consistency of his portrayal of Sue, here observes what we know anyway: that Sue was "quite unfitted by temperament and instinct to fulfill the conditions of the matrimonial relation with Phillotson, "possibly with scarce any man."

At home that evening she tells Phillotson that she "had let Mr. Fawley hold my hand a long while." Her husband seems indifferent to this news, hardly hearing her. Then she behaves very strangely in her predictably unpredictable manner: she closes herself, that night, in a stuffy, unventilated closet sooner than come to bed with her lawful husband. Phillotson, baffled, pulls open the closed door, and he finds that she had attempted to close herself in by tying the door with string, but at a pull the string breaks. Phillotson, seeing this, is very hurt: "it is monstrous that you should feel in this way." She agrees, but she can't stand him. He is very bitter, but he leaves her in peace, in the closet among mice and spiders, which she fears less than she fears her husband.

The next morning, she is silent as they have breakfast-until she suddenly asks if Phillotson would mind her living separately from him. "What was the meaning of marrying at all?" asks Phillotson, when confronted with this request. Sue tells him that she had felt honor-bound to marry him even more because she had recklessly defied **convention** and been dismissed from the training college under what appeared to be suspicious circumstances. Yet he had trusted her, accepting her word that she was innocent of all wrongdoing, and paying no attention to the rumors about her going off with Jude overnight. She loses even more respect for Phillotson when he tells her: "I am bound in honesty to tell you that I weighed its [that is, the rumor of her being Jude's mistress] probability and inquired of your cousin about it." Apparently, then, he had not trusted her implicitly. It is perhaps this knowledge which goads Sue on to hurt Phillotson. In answer to his question, "and do you mean, by living away from me, living by yourself?" Sue says: "Well, if you insisted, yes. But I meant living with Jude." Phillotson asks: "as his wife?" To which the answer is, "as I choose."

Then Sue continues: "She, or he, who lets the world, or his own portion of it, choose his plan of life for him, has no need of any other faculty than the apelike one of imitation." These are the words of John Stuart Mill. Phillotson gives the logical answer in this situation: "What do I care about J. S. Mill!" Of course, a wife quoting Mill to her husband seems fantastic under these circumstances, but as Sue's character has been presented by Hardy it is not really so unbelievable.

| Comment

John Stuart Mill (1806–73) was a British philosopher, economist, and social critic. His *Autobiography*, and the famous essay *On Liberty*, from which Sue took the above quotation, are much concerned with the rights of the individual and of those holding opinions which may not be approved by the majority of people in a given society. Mill thought that English Victorian society was too narrow, too stifling to the individual. He was especially interested in the rights of women, which had been downgraded in the Victorian era so that, however men might romanticize, the fact was that married women did not, in general, even have control legally over their own property brought to the marriage, until the Married Women's Property Acts of the 1880s and 1890s did something to alleviate this situation. One might say that *Jude the Obscure* embodies many of the ideas of John Stuart Mill, but of course Hardy was writing fiction and not social philosophy.

That Sue should actually request Phillotson to approve her going to live with her lover appears to him "a preposterous notion." Yet with her combination of artlessness and unconventionality, she can ask him this - what is more, he can't believe that the request was seriously made. Therefore, that morning Phillotson and his wife correspond by means of notes, while they are teaching in their school in adjoining classrooms. If he won't allow her to go away, will Phillotson allow Sue to live in his house "in a separate way?" He does not answer.

Her next note: "No poor woman has ever wished more than I that Eve had not fallen, so that (as the primitive Christians believed) some harmless mode of vegetation might have peopled Paradise." It is clear, then, that what Sue cannot stand is simply living a normal married life with Phillotson. But Phillotson is kind-hearted, and he finally writes back to his wife that he is "disposed to agree to your last request." And this is the arrangement that they make: that she continues to live with him, but not as man and wife.

Comment

In this chapter the break between Phillotson and Sue, which Jude has seen coming, occurs. The underlying reason for Sue's detestation of her husband is revealed: her horror of the sexual relationship with Phillotson. She didn't, indeed, know what marriage would involve, at least not fully, and her ignorance is now being paid for, by Phillotson as well as by Sue herself.

Part Fourth: Chapter Four

Phillotson is trying to interest himself once again in Roman antiquities. He and Sue are living in the same house, but as agreed previously, not as man and wife; theirs is a marriage in name only. One night, forgetting the arrangement, he enters the bedroom which is now reserved for Sue, and begins to undress- not thinking where he is. Whereupon, with a scream, Sue jumps out of the window - a second-story window. Horrified, Phillotson runs outside and finds her lying on the ground. She is, fortunately, not seriously injured, although she might have been killed by such a jump. "I was asleep and something frightened me ... a terrible dream ... I thought I saw you." She tells Phillotson this, but what is clear is that her instinct led her to prefer possible serious injury or death to remaining in the same room with her husband. When Phillotson realizes this, he is sickened-at himself, and at everything. He advises Sue to lock her door and then his morale is not helped as he realizes that she had indeed tried to lock the door but that the lock was out of order. At this point, he is described by Hardy as "a pitiable object."

Phillotson goes to call on Mr. Gillingham, his friend and schoolmate many years earlier, who also lives in the vicinity of Shaston. He confides his situation and his marital problems to Gillingham, who is aghast-more so when he hears that the staid and sober Phillotson proposes to let Sue go away with her lover. Gillingham gives the obvious response to this: "What will happen if everybody ... ", that is everybody in society, does this sort of thing? In short, Gillingham is amazed. Phillotson had struck him as conservative in all matters, and here he is calling into question the very foundations of society: the marriage-bond. Phillotson says that Sue and Jude are like two halves of one and the same person. They have an "extraordinary affinity." He can't bear to think of Sue suffering as he realizes she must be suffering if she prefers possible death or injury to him. He tells Gillingham that he is now on their side - that of Sue and Jude. What will Shaston think? wonders Gillingham. And of Sue herself he says: "I think she ought to be smacked and brought to her senses." But he does not say this out loud to his friend.

The next morning Phillotson tells Sue at breakfast that she is free to leave: she may go where she will, and be with Jude or whatever she chooses. But her husband further tells her that he'd prefer not to know her plans. As the household thus breaks up, Sue tells her husband that now that she regards him as her old teacher and as a friend, she likes him.

Their parting is very pathetic, as they discuss the breaking-up of their home. Within an hour after she leaves by train, Mr. Gillingham arrives to call on Phillotson, and learns that Sue is gone. She hasn't even taken most of her possessions, and Phillotson has the exquisitely painful task of packing them up, "to adorn her in somebody's eyes; never again in mine!"

As the chapter closes, Phillotson observes to Gillingham, in answer to the trite question: what will people think? I've gone into all that, and don't wish to argue it. I was, and am, the most old-fashioned man in the world on the question of marriage - in fact I had never thought critically about its ethics at all. But certain facts stared me in the face, and I couldn't go against them."

Comment

Phillotson, it might be said, loves his wife enough to give her her freedom, in defiance of all **convention**. In Victorian society, he, as well as Sue, will suffer for this. Gillingham represents the voice of convention-he is a man holding the fixed ideas of society on the subject of marriage. Phillotson's giving of her freedom to Sue may seem improbable, and Hardy tries to motivate it dramatically by the device of Sue's jumping out of the window. But structurally this is rather weak. Hardy tries to make the incident of Sue jumping out the window believable by making her at least half-asleep when Phillotson enters her room, for had she been fully conscious one could only attribute her action to some mental abnormality.

Part Fourth: Chapter Five

Sue has written to Jude of her break with her husband, ending with the line: "Now to our meeting!" But Jude misunderstands her, with painful results, as we shall see. A fugitive from her lawful home, though with her husband's consent, Sue meets

Jude at Melchester on the platform of the railroad station. He has packed a trunk, and tells her that his plans for them are that they will go straight on to Aldbrickham. As it is a town of some 70,000 inhabitants, nobody will notice them. He has given up his work at the cathedral also. Sue feels guilt that she has ruined his prospects in the Church and in his work - but he doesn't care; he tells her that he will never more become one of "The soldier-saints who, row on row, Burn upward, each to his point of bliss."

The quotation, incidentally, is from Robert Browning - but here Jude uses the lines of poetry ironically-for Hardy's pessimism makes him quite removed from the intellectual position of Robert Browning in terms especially of the hopes to which a man may validly hold in an age where scientific determinism, as reflected certainly in *Jude the Obscure*, had undermined for many the truths of orthodox Christian belief.

Now Jude tells Sue that he is ashamed of having hated Phillotson for marrying her. Sue says that while she admires Phillotson's "large-mindedness" she still can't stand him, and the last thing she would wish to do is live with Phillotson ever again as his wife. She says, though, that she would never have run away from Phillotson; she has acted only because he had given her permission to leave. But there are further complications in the relationship between Sue and Jude, for as they are waiting for the train, Jude impulsively kisses Sue - and unexpectedly she asks, in fact she implores him, not to kiss her again. Jude then tells her, perhaps subconsciously as a punishment, that Arabella has written him asking for a divorce, as she wants to marry her Australian "husband," in order to legalize their relationship. This concern about legality on the part of Arabella may be surprising, for she had never seemed to care for such things before, but the truth is that since she is now in the same country, England, with both of the men she has married, she could be found out and, as the guilty party, receive a prison sentence for bigamy. And Jude could bring this about at any time simply by denouncing her to the authorities. She trusts him not to do this, despite the several injuries she had inflicted on him over the years. But Jude has agreed to give Arabella the divorce, as he tells Sue at this point.

Jude and Sue are booked for a single room that night at (ironically) the Temperance Hotel at Aldbrickham. Sue is fearful, telling Jude that she didn't expect this-she didn't expect, to be blunt, that he would wish to have any sexual relationship with her. What can he say: "Have it as you wish!" What Sue appears to be trying to say is that while he is her lover, she is frigid physically toward him as, it may be, she is toward all men.

Comment

Much of the dialogue of the chapter proceeds by circumlocution and innuendo-in fact, this is true of much of the book. As Hardy's frankest statement of his critique of Victorian marriage, the novel was very strong indeed for his contemporaries, as evidenced by the storm of objections raised when the book appeared. But many readers today find the implications of the dialogue both flat and somewhat prurient. But Hardy, given the **conventions** of his era, had to imply much more concerning the truth of the relationship between men and women than he could state directly, or it is probably that his books would not have been permitted to be sold at all, except clandestinely.

As Jude thinks of Sue's attitude, he remembers the ill-fated Christ-minster undergraduate, who had been, so to speak, tortured to death by Sue in much the same manner as she is now treating him. "Crucify me if you will!" Jude says to Sue. She is still sophisticated about most things, but is a child in some, including especially her relationship to Jude in particular and men in general. She seems to have learned nothing from her ill-fated marriage to Phillotson, while Jude, on the contrary, had at least learned from his marriage to Arabella that the merely animal alone could never satisfy him. It turns out that the inn they go to at Aldbrickham-not the Temperance Hotel, to which Sue objects-is the very same one at which Jude and Arabella stayed. Again, by a fantastic coincidence, the waiting-maid speaks to Sue in Jude's temporary absence, and remembers the fact that Jude had stayed there with a different woman, Arabella, two months previously. Sue confronts Jude with this; she is very upset. Jude explains everything, but she says: "It was treacherous of you to have her again!" He insists that after all Arabella was his legal wife at the time, and that he could hardly have been thought false to Sue, as she was the wife of another. This chapter, a fantasy from the point of view of sexual psychology, ends with Sue's quoting an ethereal poem of Shelley, *Epipsychidion:*

There was a Being whom my spirit oft Met on its visioned wanderings far aloft ....

In short, she wishes that Jude would be her Shelleyan soulmate, but she shrinks from the physical relationship. As they bid each other good night, Sue is still Jude's in all things, but she will not yield to him as his mistress, which is what Jude desires, seeing himself now as another pathetic successor to Sue's Christminster undergraduate.

Comment

This chapter seems improbable to many modern readers, especially those nurtured on what may well be such excessive frankness for its own sake in literature as to amount to outright pornography - though this line is difficult to draw. In view of the character of Sue as Hardy has gradually revealed it, we are not surprised at Sue's bizarre behavior towards Jude. Sue would be called in today's terms a sexual neurotic, and this chapter highlights the unfolding of her neurosis under the stress of her leaving her husband and her flight with Jude.

Part Fourth: Chapter Six

Phillotson, still teaching at his school in his native town of Shaston, continues his routine. His wife's absence is not at first noticed, as her place has been taken in the school by another young woman. But after a month, some talk begins, and Phillotson's honesty and directness will not permit him to equivocate about what has become of his wife. Thus, the head of the School Committee speaks to him, and is amazed at what he is told: that Phillotson has sanctioned his wife's leaving him to run away with her lover. "I was not her jailer," he says. Gossip starts. Presently Phillotson comes to see his friend Gillingham, telling him of the School Committee's decision about his case: "They have requested me to send in my resignation on account of my scandalous conduct in giving my tortured wife her liberty- or, as they call it, condoning her adultery. But I shan't resign." Gillingham suggests that he change his mind and resign, for his own good. But he refuses, and is summarily dismissed from his position. Phillotson then calls a public meeting to attempt to justify position he has taken. Everyone is against him, except a miscellaneous group of circus and fair performers who, in the absence of work, are out for some fun. And they will have their fun at Phillotson's expense, for a slight scuffle takes place at the meeting, and a clergyman receives a bloody nose from "an emancipated chimney-sweep." Phillotson feels, as well he may, so degraded by this event that he becomes seriously ill. Gillingham, who has been and still is a true friend, decides that the best thing he can do for Phillotson is to write Sue an anonymous note of her husband's illness. She of course does not even know that he has been dismissed from his job because of his generosity towards her. Three days later Sue, without even now realizing the latter fact, arrives from Aldbrickham. He is moved at seeing her. "You are an odd creature," he says to his wife. "The idea of your coming to see me after what has passed!" Gillingham is amazed when he hears that Sue has been back, and further, that Phillotson proposes to dissolve the legal tie which still binds him to Sue, so that she can have her freedom and not be persecuted by society.

Gillingham respects his friend for holding the opinions he does with consistency, though at the same time Gillingham in no way agrees with him. As the chapter ends, therefore, both Phillotson and Jude are planning to grant divorces to their legal wives, from quite different motives.

Comment

It should be noted that divorce was very difficult to obtain in 1890 in England. Only an act of Parliament, the result in most cases of a private bill brought by a Member of Parliament on behalf of a supporter or constituent, could finally dissolve a marriage. And, as might be expected, this was an expensive legal process. Generally, only the wealthy could afford such a thing as divorce, while too often the "poor man's divorce" was simply to flee from his spouse-desertion. Other novels, for example Dickens's *Hard Times*, earlier in the century, and George Meredith's *The Amazing Marriage*, used marriage and divorce, especially the abuses of the divorce laws, as central **themes** in this period - but Hardy's dwelling on the subject is the most unreservedly gloomy, and most conspicuous in *Jude the Obscure*.

In Part Fourth it is, then, marriage and divorce, or marriage as an imperfect institution in his society, which Hardy chooses to criticize as he shows the baleful effects of what we would call incompatibility and sexual neurosis in the cases of Phillotson and Sue. Marriage, which of course is assumed to be the basis of the family and of society, is atrocious in its effects on Sue especially. Thus, Part Fourth begins with the quotation from Milton's writings on divorce, and ends with divorce.

Part Fourth is perhaps the most unsuccessful of the six major divisions of this novel, from the point of view of art-of the technique of fiction and the believability (verisimilitude) of the treatment of its principal characters. The symbols of this part: the killing of the trapped rabbit, the physical decadence of the medieval town of Shaston, the burning by Jude of his religious books, the strange, bizarre behavior of Sue towards her husband, and the interest of Phillotson in obscure Roman antiquities-all of these present the picture of objects from which life is departing or has departed, so that only the outward and unvital aspect is left, not the spirit. All of these things seem to symbolize the loss of vitality in those institutions which Hardy has chosen to satirize in Jude, but primarily marriage, and secondarily the Church, which considers marriage, at least Christian marriage, indissoluble and of sacramental importance. Here Hardy presents marriage not as sacrament, but rather as a sacrifice, in which one of both parties (as in the cases of Sue and Phillotson) suffer terribly.

But in his eagerness to illustrate his critique of marriage, Hardy loads the dice, as it were, against Sue and Phillotson, especially in Part Fourth. Phillotson seems lacking in common sense, and somehow even his renunciation of Sue does not seem particularly noble or altruistic. Sue is preposterous here, especially in (a) Her jumping out of the window in Chapter Four, and (b) In her running off with Jude, and then refusing to live with him. She weakens Hardy's argument. One cannot in fairness say that Hardy is against marriage per se, but he is certainly against the possible abuses inherent in the married state. But as he presents Sue, she is so far removed from the bounds of normality, especially in this part, that what we have is a grotesque portrait of one who seems absolutely fated to be terribly unhappy. Sue is the picture of one driven to fanaticism and madness, but despite what Hardy implies about an unwise marriage as being the cause of her troubles, the reader is left with the impression that Sue's troubles stem not from the blighting effects of her marriage but from her own character, which renders her incapable of happiness in marriage. Character is destiny-here, Sue's character is her destiny, but it is an unbelievable character. In Part Fifth, we are to see the further effect of her character on those who are close to her.

JUDE THE OBSCURE

TEXTUAL ANALYSIS

PART FIFTH

Part Fifth ("At Aldbrickham And Elsewhere"): Chapter One

The epigraph which begins this part is from the Roman emperor and great Stoic philosopher Marcus Aurelius Antoninus: "Thy aerial part, and all the fiery parts which are mingled in thee, though by nature they have an upward tendency, still in obedience to the disposition of the universe they are overpowered here in the compound mass the body."

The relevance of this quotation is to the dualism of body and spirit, of intellect and emotion, especially as in *Jude the Obscure* these are objectified in the persons of Jude and Sue. Both embody dualism, which as a philosophical term is defined generally as a philosophical system that recognizes the existence of two opposing qualities each of which is of primary importance. The dualities may be those of mind and body, or other pairs of primary but opposing qualities. And dualism is most strongly found, among the characters in the novel, in Jude. Sue is all spirit or intellect, in unstable relation with the physical body. Jude, on the other hand, is a balance of the physical and the intellectual, with the physical periodically, in Hardy's view of him, dragging him down from those realms of intellectual accomplishment which he had sought to master.

As this chapter opens, a number of months have elapsed since Sue and Jude had gone away together. They are living at Aldbrickham-living together in a little house rented by Jude and furnished with Aunt Drusilla's old furniture which Jude had inherited. But they are not living together physically as lovers; Sue and Jude are in the same curious relationship of unsatisfied passion on Jude's part as had been the case between Sue and Christminster undergraduate with whom she had also lived. There is legal terminology here which requires explanation - "the decree nisi in the case of Phillotson versus Phillotson and Fawley, pronounced six months ago, has just been made absolute." So Sue says to Jude, as we see them in their house at the beginning of this chapter.

A decree nisi is a divorce decree "unless." It is roughly what the law in some states of the United States calls an interlocutory, as opposed to a final, divorce decree. Apparently Sue's husband is suing Sue for divorce, on grounds of adultery, and though the word is not mentioned here in this chapter we can tell that these are the grounds, because a co-respondent has been named in the suit: Fawley. A decree nisi would be made absolute, or final, after a stated period, unless it was contested-here the period is six months, and now Sue is no longer Phillotson's wife. And this was a fairly unusual proceeding in Hardy's age, at least before the First World War, especially since adultery was one of the few grounds for such a legal proceedings, and at least one party would then be publicly branded as an adulterer or adulteress. It is ironic that in such a legal proceeding the truth has not been told here - the law assumes that Jude and Sue are living in an adulterous relationship, whereas the truth is that they are not. "If the truth about us had been known, the decree wouldn't have been pronounced," says Sue, bitter about what she considers the hypocrisy of society. But the fact is that justly or otherwise, Sue and Jude are finally free to marry. Jude's divorce decree nisi has also been made absolute, we learn, and Jude has proposed that he and Sue marry as soon as possible. But Sue is still cold to this idea; she says, "I suppose so," for she is still horrified that she should be the property of a man, "licensed to be loved on the premises by you-Ugh, how horrible and sordid!" Her view of marriage, in short, has not changed. She speculates further about marriage, and seems even more bitter about it as an institution than she has been in the past: it is foreign to a man's nature to go on loving a person when he is told that he must ... ." Most reasonable people would say that in describing the legal marriage tie in these terms, Sue distorts the institution out of all recognition. But evidently she believes this about marriage. She assumes that many women pretend that they wish to be married; they enter into it "for the dignity it is assumed to confer."

Jude finally tells her that she needn't worry; she doesn't have to marry him or to become his mistress if she doesn't wish to. As the chapter ends, they are still living in the curious relationship, more than friends, but not physically lovers. Sue is helping Jude with his stone-cutting; he is supporting them by cutting and lettering headstones. And this is a lower class of work for him than his former trade of cathedral masonry, but he earns enough to support them thereby.

Comment

This chapter is fairly self-evident, except for some of the legal terminology. Sue is still denying Jude full possession of her, and is not anxious to marry him. She is unable to realize that a man with Jude's passionate nature is tortured by such an incomplete relationship; that he is generously giving up much, if not everything, including his career, for her. But the relationship, whatever Sue may think, is basically unstable. It needs only a spark to set Jude afire, and that spark will come shortly.

Part Fifth: Chapter Two

The spark comes in the form of a visit from Arabella. Sue receives her in the absence of Jude, and recognizes her on sight: "a fleshy, coarse woman," Sue calls her. The woman had not given her name to Sue. Sue is miserable, as she tells Jude of the mysterious visit. That same evening, there is a knock at the door. Looking out the window, Jude sees a woman. It is indeed Arabella. She tells him that she is in trouble, and has no one to turn to-she has "a sudden responsibility that has been sprung on me from Australia." What this is, she will not say. But Jude feels sorry for her, and says that he must do her the kindness of hearing what she has to tell him, though Sue is frantic that he not do this. "It is only to entrap you," Sue tells him of Arabella's actions. "She's not your wife," says Sue. But Jude reminds her, rather cuttingly: "But you are not either, dear, yet." Despite Sue's wishes, Jude goes out to speak with Arabella. But she has already gone, thinking he has rebuffed her. Sue had been afraid that Jude would go with Arabella to a bar and get drunk, or be made drunk by her, but he hasn't done this. As he comes back to Sue, he tells her of the difficulties of their situation and the superhuman self-control demanded continually on his part, and demanded of one who is certainly not by nature an ascetic.

Sue agrees, at this time, that she will become Jude's lover; the implication in this chapter is that on the night of Arabella's appearance Sue indeed gives herself to Jude, fearful that she will lose him otherwise. Jude tells her that he will arrange for their marriage as soon as possible; the banns will have to be posted, but he will see to that. Sue recognizes that she has been precipitated into agreement principally by the rivalry with Arabella, and feels contrite-it is also, to her, a wrong motive for agreeing to marry. "The little bird is caught at last!" she says sorrowfully to Jude. She is in a contrite mood, and when she is thus, she is ascetically inclined and seems to wish to be punished. As Jude goes out, Sue waits for a while and then leaves the house herself, heading for the public house where she knows that Arabella is staying. Arabella has not yet left, and Sue sends up word that she would like to see her. Arabella had been expecting Jude, and is put out that the visitor is Sue.

As they are about to talk-Arabella having discerned that when she had last seen Sue, Jude had not yet possessed Sue, but that in the interval this had come about - a telegram arrives for Arabella, which she opens and reads instantly. It is from her Australian, now running a pub in Lambeth. He wants Arabella to return to him. Arabella seems triumphant at this turn of events; apparently the man had thrown her out and beaten her while he had been drinking, but now he is penitent and thinks that Arabella is good for his pub's business, as she well may be. So Arabella is all ready to leave, but she cannot resist giving some advice to Sue: that Sue ought to see to it that Jude marries her as soon as possible, if she is wise. She adds: "Never such a tender fool as Jude, if a woman seems in trouble, and coaxes him a bit!" Arabella knows this essential kindliness of Jude. After all, she has traded on it for years. But as she thinks that her own problems are settled, Arabella says that she would advise Sue "to get the business legally done as soon as possible."

Sue is repelled by Arabella's cynical coarseness, and shows it. Arabella's insulting statement to Sue as they part hastily is: "Bolted from your first, [i.e. first husband] didn't you, like me?" Arabella tells her that she wishes to see Jude before she leaves, but as she sees this is not possible, Sue wishing to prevent such a meeting, she will write instead about a little matter of business.

Comment

In this chapter Sue finally has become Jude's mistress, Hardy tells us indirectly. Arabella instinctively perceives this, and in turn this tells her that the relationship between Jude and Sue cannot be a completely happy one, at least as far as Jude is concerned. She, Arabella, knows Jude too well.

Sue's motive in agreeing to be Jude's lover and to marry him is the rather ignoble one of jealousy, with the natural fear that she will lose Jude to Arabella. Sue's decision then is made on essentially negative considerations: fear, jealousy, a sense of insecurity; not really love for Jude. This point is debatable, but Hardy seems to present Sue in other than an ideal light here.

Part Fifth: Chapter Three

Sue is worried about the nature of the news which Arabella wishes to communicate to Jude via the letter she mentioned. When she returns home sees Jude, therefore, he can sense that she is preoccupied with something. But he does not ask her, as he respects her right to her private thoughts. Sue further admits, even though Jude has not asked her, that she is beginning to have some sympathy for Arabella - and further, that Arabella's fate has more than ever convinced her "how hopelessly vulgar an institution legal marriage is." One of the things which horrifies her about marriage, or so she says, is the legal compulsion to be responsive to a man. Also, as Arabella had said to her matter-of-factly, it is easier for the woman in an unsatisfactory marriage relationship to take legal action against her husband, putting him in prison if necessary, than it is for a woman who is simply living with a man without benefit of clergy. At any rate, Sue predicts that once Jude is legally her husband, he will be cold toward her and the compulsion inherent in the marriage relationship will ruin them both.

These gloomy thoughts, occasioned by the unexpected visit to Arabella, lead to a dreamy delay in their preparations for the marriage ceremony. Three weeks later, the banns have still not been posted. Meanwhile, though their own marriage has not taken place, Arabella has been wasting no time. A newspaper arrives from Arabella, announcing Arabella's marriage to Cartlett, the innkeeper whom she had bigamously married in Australia. Now Arabella is legally the wife of this man. She would seem incapable of injuring Jude any longer, except ... that with the newspaper Arabella sends along a letter addressed to Jude. And the news is perfectly stunning to Jude. Arabella informs him that there had been a boy born of the marriage to Jude, eight months after Arabella had left Jude originally and was living with her parents at Sydney. She claims that the facts are easily provable; Arabella claims that she had become pregnant by Jude just as they had separated, and at the time she was leaving for Australia she hadn't known that she was going to bear Jude's child. At this point, the boy is still in Australia living with Arabella's parents. But they have written her saying that now that both Arabella and Jude are in England, it would be appreciated if one of them would take the boy off the hands of the parents. Arabella continues to swear that the boy is lawfully Jude's although Jude has his doubts; he knows Arabella's character rather too well to be sure of such things. But he adds: "It hit me hard!" The electrifying news hit Sue hard also; she feels sorry for the boy, as she realizes that he is wanted by no one, least of all by Arabella and her Australian husband. And this sympathy will prove ultimately disastrous to both Jude and Sue.

They decide to ask Arabella to have him sent to them, and plan to make a home for the boy and to marry after all. A few weeks later, a pale and wizened little boy appears on the Aldbrickham railway station platform, where Sue and Jude are waiting to meet him. It is the child of Arabella and Jude, and from his manner, he is "Age masquerading as Juvenility." Sue looks at the boy closely, and decides that he looks like Jude, and therefore that Arabella had been telling the truth as to the paternity of the child. But what Jude cannot stand, and even more, what Sue cannot stand about the boy is that he is half Arabella's child. As the chapter closes, we find the characterization of the boy to be perfectly fantastic, for he is not believable as a child-he seems incredibly old and long-suffering. It is, it bears repeating, this quality of incredible suffering in the boy which leads Sue to suggest finally, and against her better judgment, that she and Jude marry.

Comment

It was the character of the child of Jude and Arabella which led to the greatest outcry about this novel when it first appeared - this quality of somber fantasy surrounding the boy was perceived as totally lacking in verisimilitude. As Hardy further develops the character of the boy in the chapters which immediately follow, he becomes even more fantastic, until it is clear that he is not even meant by Hardy to resemble a real human being, but rather that he is a symbol. But a symbol of what? This remains to be established, as it is in the chapters which follow.

The other aspect of this chapter which gives the reader pause as being insufficiently motivated dramatically or structurally is the fact that now that Sue and Jude are legally free to marry, they hesitate. Their procrastination on this matter is not really understandable - they set out to have the banns of marriage published, but then simply and by default decide not to bother for a time. It is as though they are living a charmed life, within a magic circle - and stepping outside the circle, which is what marriage will mean, is threatening and sinister for them, more so than the fact of their not being married is threatening, even though they continue to incur the wrath of society.

Part Fifth: Chapter Four

The character of Jude's curious son unfolds further in this chapter, and at the outset we are convinced that Hardy intended that the boy should be a symbol; the question is whether he is an effective or a mechanical and clumsy symbol, and many readers and critics in Hardy's age and thereafter have thought the latter. For Jude and Sue, now that they have the boy home, are not even able to find out his name, if he has a name.

But he was never christened, "because, if I died in damnation, 't would save the expense of a Christian funeral." So the boy says, and this is such an awful thought, and would have been to many of Hardy's contemporaries, that the character of the boy is made grotesque thereby. Since he was never christened, he has no name: "Little Father Time is what they always called me-it is a nickname-because I look so aged, they say." Jude and Sue, shocked by what they perceive as the callousness of the treatment of the boy by Arabella, his own mother, decide that they will marry, and have Little Father Time christened the day they are married. They publish the banns of their marriage - the notice of intention to marry which is a public notice so that any person knowing a reason why they should not be married may come forward with such information - and apply for the civil license to marry at the registry office. And occasionally Sue walks by the office, seeing affixed to the wall outside "the notice of the purported clinch of their union."

It appears that the wedding will take place, if for no other reason than that Sue and Jude wish to be legally married for the sake of Little Father Time. Jude decides that he will invite the only person remaining on earth who knew him during his early life at Marygreen, the widow Edlin, who had tended Aunt Drusilla in her last illness. Presently the elderly Mrs. Edlin arrives, bringing presents and a word of comfort, for she hopes that this time the marriage will work out, even despite the unfortunate history of the Fawley family. But in saying this, she tells Jude and Sue something neither of them had known - a melodramatic tale of an ancestor of theirs who had been hanged just on the brow of the hill by the Brown house, near the milestone between Marygreen and Alfredston. He had been hanged because after his wife left him, and their child died, he had stolen the body in its coffin and been hanged for burglary, under the harsh English criminal law of the preceding century-while his wife had gone mad after he was dead.

As they hear the macabre story, a small voice is heard: it comes from little Time. "If I was you, mother, I wouldn't marry father." The story has upset them all, and the next morning, as Sue asks Jude to kiss her as a lover, since once they are married he will never do so, she thinks, she says that she feels "as if a tragic doom overhung our family, as it did the house of Atreus." That same morning, they start for the Registry Office to be married, accompanied by their only witness, the Widow Edlin.

The surroundings at the said office are sordid and depressing. They see, as they wait their turn, a young soldier being apparently forced into marrying a girl who is heavily pregnant - the girl also has a black eye, and it turns out the she had just met the young man at the door of the jail where he had been incarcerated. The other couples waiting ahead of Jude and Sue are no more appealing, and the place gives Sue the horrors. She doesn't want to go through with the ceremony, and despite her religious views, or rather her agnosticism, she now prefers to be married in a church. They both walk away from the office, as though they had committed a misdemeanor.

Comment

It is in this chapter, after the reluctance of Sue to go through with the marriage at the Registry Office, that the delay in the marriage of Sue and Jude strikes some readers as fantastic. Indeed the delay is only believable if one treats the situation as one which Hardy was setting up for symbolic purposes involving his attack on what he saw as the abuses of marriage. Sue's delay otherwise is exasperating-her continual talk, her dissatisfaction with almost everything she sees and hears in the conduct of other ordinary people. We fully understand at this point what D.H. Lawrence meant when he wrote: "One of the supremest products of our civilization is Sue, and a product that well frightens us."

Upon leaving the Registry Office, still not legally married, Sue and Jude visit a church where a wedding is in progress, just to see how the ceremony appears to them by contrast with the civil ceremony they had refused to go through. Sue observes that "it really does seem immoral in me to go and undertake the same thing again with open eyes ...I feel doubts of-my being proof against the sordid conditions of a business contract again."

After additional talk about the nature of the marriage contract, Sue and Jude come, by slightly different lines of reasoning, to the same conclusion: "that for us particular two an irrevocable oath is risky. Then, Jude, let us go home without killing our dream!" The common enemy is "coercion." When they return to their house, they tell the Widow Edlin that they have not yet made up their minds about marriage, but that they would like to keep this information from the boy, Father Time. "If we are happy as we are, what does it matter to anybody?"

Comment

While Sue's line of argument against marriage is extremely one-sided, and in this chapter becomes to the modern reader somewhat fantastic and pointless, it is necessary to take a historical perspective on this argument. Sue reflects the thinking of feminists of the stamp of Mary Wollstonecraft and her daughter, Mary Shelley, second wife of the great poet-in fact Shelley, who shared with his wife certain unorthodox ideas about marriage, is mentioned or quoted several times in *Jude the Obscure*. Women did not receive the vote in Great Britain until after the conclusion of the First World War, and in other ways were legally in an inferior status to men - and this was especially evident in Hardy's time in the legal implications of the contract of marriage, for of course civil marriage, by the time Hardy wrote *Jude the Obscure*, was a contract. And it is the contract which makes Sue frantic in her reluctance to be bound legally by ties which she believes can never be made subject to legislation. She believes this as a militant feminist, ready to incur the wrath of society which would not condone such an irregular union as the one into which she has entered with Jude.

Part Fifth: Chapter Five

In June, the year unspecified because of Hardy's wish to universalize his subject, Jude, Sue, and Little Father Time are in the town of some nine or ten thousand people in Upper Wessex which Hardy calls here Stoke-Barehills, and which in actuality is the town of Basingstoke. It is at the time of the Great Wessex Agricultural Show, and many visitors and sightseers are in town, together with the kind of people who follow the crowd in order to separate the people from their money. In fact, one of these is the same charlatan, Physician Vilbert, who had earlier helped Arabella trap Jude into marrying her, back at Marygreen. An excursion train arrives from London on a certain day during the agricultural show, and a man and a woman appear on the railway station platform. The woman is Arabella, and the man her new legally-married husband, the Australian barman named Cartlett. Cartlett, the landlord of The Three Horns, Lambeth, has been drinking, as evidenced by his thickened speech. Almost immediately upon their arrival, they see a man, woman, and child on the station platform, and Arabella is astonished to see that the man is none other than Jude.

Arabella has a sudden covetous feeling toward the boy, Little Father Time, as she sees him; this despite the fact that she had ignored his existence for years and has been only too glad to see him sent to Jude and Sue. Since Jude and Sue are walking close, hand-in-hand, Arabella concludes that they are "only lovers, or lately married." Hardy cannot resist another dig at the formal marriage relationship here; he uses once again the most improbable coincidence to bring the central characters into close proximity. Arabella is sure that they are not married, since Sue sticks so close to Jude. Since Cartlett is indifferent, and to do him credit sees it as no business of his to follow Jude and Sue, Arabella and Cartlett part for the afternoon, arranging to meet at a refreshment tent later.

Again by outrageous coincidence, Arabella meets her girlhood friend, Anny, of the times back at the pig-keeper's house. She has not seen Anny for years-nor has she seen Physician Vilbert, who likewise by coincidence turns up at the same time. Now all the principals in the action which had involved Arabella and Jude in marriage so long ago have appeared, all in one place, by chance. And now, their lives are to become intertwined once again, though at the moment none of them, but least of all Jude, suspects this. Meanwhile, Jude and Sue, with the boy, are looking at a model, with the lettering: "Model of Cardinal College, Christminster; by J. Fawley and S.F.M. Bridehead." To the practical Arabella, it seems that Jude is still attending to matters extraneous to his business, which is stone-cutting. Arabella still thinks of Jude and Sue as "silly fools." She follows them, nevertheless. Meanwhile, her trusty friend Anny has mentioned to Physician Vilbert that she thinks Arabella is still interested in her first husband, which is indeed the case. Vilbert offers Arabella, when he sees her, a love-potion made of doves' hearts; she pays him five shillings for the vial of this concoction. Then she finds her husband, Cartlett, and they greet each other in their usual surly manner, "and they left the tent together, this pot-bellied man and florid woman, in the antipathetic, recriminatory mood of the average husband and wife of Christendom." Jude and Sue, with Little Father Time, are fascinated by the tinted roses in the place where the flowers are on display - they stand in the midst of the roses, to the point where they seem almost a part of nature at its most beautiful - and the chapter closes with this symbolic tableau.

Comment

The inner meaning of this chapter may be said to be expressed by two contrasting symbols. The first has already been referred to: the unusual and beautiful tinted roses, with Jude and Sue and the young boy in their midst contemplating them. The roses symbolize perhaps the unspoiled freshness of nature, and of life lived in conformity with nature. Nature is "forever young and still to be enjoyed," and Jude and Sue are of it as long as they do not succumb to the disease of too much idle thought and reflection. Father Time enters this tableau as a withering force; he likes the beauty of the roses, but says: "I... keep on thinking they'd all be withered in a few days!"

The second symbol may be found in the account by the quack physician, Vilbert, of his method of preparation of his fraudulent love-potion. Doves, of course, are a symbol of love, and the barbarous process he relates to Arabella (whether he is lying or not makes little difference; most likely his "love-potion" is simply clear water) symbolically involves the killing of love, which is represented by Sue and Jude, by the world, which is represented by Arabella, Anny, Physician Vilbert, and Arabella's raw and unpleasing husband, Cartlett. At least, the occurrence of the love-potion and the roses in this chapter seems to be justified, if at all, more on symbolic than on literal grounds.

PART FIFTH: CHAPTER SIX

In the neighborhood where Sue and Jude are living, there is beginning to be talk about them. After all, they are a young couple, but it is known that each has been divorced and that a boy who seems rather old to be theirs is living with them as their son, and who calls Jude "Father" and Sue "Mother." Remarks are made to the boy at school which, when Jude and Sue hear them, cause them a great deal of pain. So they go off to London for a few days, shortly after they had withdrawn from the attempt at marriage in London, and upon their return they let it be understood indirectly that they are at last legally married. But this still does not dispel the atmosphere of scandal which surrounds them. They are snubbed by such worthies as the baker's lad and the neighboring wives of workmen; and worse, Jude's business suffers, as the orders for his work begin to fall off.

Jude will have to return to journeyman-work again, and this is inconvenient as it pays less than having his own business. Further, he still owes money as a result of the court costs attendant upon his divorce. But just as Jude is downhearted about his business affairs, he is asked to do a commission at a little country church: restoring and relettering the stone-work of the Ten Commandments which adorn the church.

Jude makes an agreement to do the work, and visits the church. Sue comes to help with the lettering. The vicar and churchwarden seem surprised to see a woman assisting with such work. There is recognition of Jude and Sue by a number of local women, including the woman who cleans the church, and gossip immediately starts again. "A strange pair to be painting the Two Tables!" This leads to the telling of a long, gossipy story of the painting of the Ten Commandments on a church outside Gaymead, which is near the present church. This was over a hundred years ago, and at that time true religion had been remiss in Gaymead, so that a number of the men showed up drunk to the work. But they fell down senseless, and when they awakened, it was in the midst of a thunder-storm, and by the flashes of lightning they "seemed to see in the gloom a dark figure with very thin legs and a curious voot" who stood on the ladder and finished the work. The next morning they saw that all the "nots" were left out of the Ten Commandments, to the great scandal of the entire congregation. The bishop was sent for to reconsecrate the church. This story, of course, is told in the full hearing of Jude and Sue. Jude tells Sue, "never mind." But she says that she cannot bear such treatment by a society which thinks people wicked because they have chosen to live their own way.

The contractor Willis, the man who had employed Jude on this job, appears and asks them to leave the work-he seems rather embarrassed, and offers to pay Jude for the week. But he has had a complaint that they are not fit persons to do such lettering on such a sacred subject as the Ten Commandments. "I ought not to have come!" says Sue, pathetically, as Jude picks up his tools. Jude doesn't blame the contractor Willis, who has his own reputation to take care of - but he does blame a society which persecutes him, as he thinks, for opinions he holds even though they injure nobody else. Meanwhile Jude has joined an Artisans' Mutual Improvement Society-something which took the place of formal educational institutions for workingmen in England at that period, and has been placed on a committee of the society. But when he appears at a meeting a few evenings after his dismissal from the church job, he hears some pointed remarks, directed at him, about "a common standard of conduct." He resigns immediately.

They decide to move from their lodgings and go away, but first they hold an auction of their furniture, principally that which Jude had inherited from his Aunt Drusilla. The auction is very painful, primarily because there are many remarks made by those present not about the furniture, but about Jude and Sue. The final item of sale is two pairs of pigeons, and these perhaps are related to the symbolism of the doves in Chapter Five above. They are sold to a poulterer, who will place them in his shop for sale as food. Sue cannot stand this thought, and that evening she goes down and opens the hamper by the poulterer's shop door, and lets them fly away. When Sue goes home, she tells Jude what she has done, and observes: "Oh why should Nature's law be mutual butchery!" And that statement, though made over a relatively trivial incident, is important because it is the clearest one-sentence statement of the **theme** of *Jude the Obscure:* "Oh why should Nature's law be mutual butchery!"

| Comment

Chapter Six is intended to show the way society unjustly persecutes those who do not adhere to its laws-unjustly, that is, Hardy's frame of reference. Jude and Sue are not physically hurt, but society shows itself to be at once small-minded and relentless as it pursues them, deprives Jude of his means of earning a living, and in general treats Sue and Jude as trapped animals much as the pigeons are trapped in the cage in the poulterer's shop. But while Sue releases the birds, nobody releases Jude or herself. "Perhaps we have 'done that which was right in our own eyes.'" says Jude. But as this chapter implies, the morale of the little family is beginning to erode under the persecution of society, which no man or woman can fully ignore, Hardy believed; those in his novels who are completely living to themselves alone prove only that this cannot be done.

Part Fifth: Chapter Seven

Jude and Sue are no longer to be seen in Aldbrickham. They have moved on, entering by choice a nomadic kind of existence far from their previous haunts. Jude does "freestone" jobs, carrying each to completion as a sort of independent contractor responsible only to each customer, and then he and Sue move on. He is, as we know, a good workman, and is able to earn a living for his family by this means.

For two and a half years they live this roving but not unpleasant life. Sue is a mother by Jude; they have two children, and are expecting another. Their wanderings take them to many towns, although they stay away from such familiar places as Christminster. Hardy tells us that Jude has been changing in his mental outlook, becoming more skeptical - "hardly a shred of the beliefs with which he had first gone up to Christminster now remaining with him." He has, of course, by this time dropped his idea of a career in the Church, and in fact can hardly see how or why he had originally hoped for such a career.

On a Saturday evening in May, three years after Arabella and Cartlett had seen Jude and Sue at the agricultural show, two women appear at the spring fair at Kennetbridge, and take a room at a "temperance inn," which is an inn that does not sell or serve liquor. The women are Anny, and Arabella, the latter dressed in the deep mourning of a widow. We find very quickly that Arabella's husband, Cartlett, has died, and that Arabella has evidently come to town because she has traced the whereabouts of Jude and Sue, and wants to see Jude. She also wants to see her son, who by now believes that Sue is his natural mother. Sue is, as Arabella speaks with her in Jude's absence, keeping a stall with cakes and gingerbreads. It is a business that will lead a meager living, even at the season of the spring fair. Arabella remarks as much, saying that she is surprised to see the circumstances in which Jude and Sue are now living. Sue is selling what she calls "Christminster cakes" of gingerbread; Jude has gotten this idea from his early work as a boy with Aunt Drusilla's bakery. They are a fast-selling item at the fair. Apparently Jude is ill, and this has led him to give up his stone-work.

Arabella speaks to Sue from a plane of moral superiority, telling her that she, Arabella, had undergone a religious conversion after Cartlett's untimely death. But Arabella's selfishness, moral obtuseness, and other less admirable qualities peep through her talk, and it is clear that she is tracing Jude because she is interested in having him back, if possible, despite her former callous treatment of him and of her son.

| Comment

Here the contrast between Sue's character and Arabella's is further developed. This dramatic revelation of character is in support of Hardy's thesis as expressed in this novel that the selfish and wicked, such as Arabella, prosper, and the children of light-Sue and Jude-are defeated by their own good natures and their innocence, as well as by life. And this is essentially a religious idea; it is of the stuff of dramatic tragedy of the highest order: Job, or *Oedipus Rex*, or *Hamlet*, although it is open to question now *Jude the Obscure* ranks as tragedy in comparison with these. But we can see that the last, tragic action of the novel is being prepared by the author in this chapter.

Part Fifth: Chapter Eight

Coincidence now plays its incredible part in the novel, as we have learned to expect. Arabella wants Jude back, and is frank with herself, while slightly shocking her friend Anny, by saying this. "I'd take him from her if I could!" says Arabella of Jude. She recognizes and frankly confronts her feelings, which is the one thing Arabella can do which Sue cannot. As Arabella and Anny talk, they are driving in a horse and cart toward Alfredston. In the road, they see an elderly man carrying a basket, and offer him a lift. He turns out to be Richard Phillotson, older and more worn. By this point, we scarcely pay attention to the utter improbability of such a meeting. But it is essential from the point of view of the prospective action.

Phillotson and Arabella, after refreshing their memories about each other, talk about their marriages. Arabella finds out that after all this time, Phillotson's life has come in a complete circle: he is keeping the school at Marygreen just as he had done many years ago, and keeping it on sufferance, at fifty pounds a year. Arabella points out that Phillotson was wrong about Sue; he had believed the story that Sue had committed adultery with Jude, but the truth is that she was innocent. This Arabella tells him, for her own reasons. "She'd have come round in time." So Arabella speaks of Sue to her former husband. She tells him how hard it has been for Sue: innocent or guilty, she says, it is always the woman who pays! She gives him further advice, for though he is a presumably learned schoolmaster, Arabella is infinitely more cunning in the ways of the world. And she does put ideas into Richard Phillotson's head.

Jude is ill-his appearance indicates that he has passed through a severe illness, probably a bout with tuberculosis, or as it was called then, consumption, because of the wasting action of the disease. Persons who worked with stone, as well as miners and others working in damp surroundings, were especially prone to have trouble with their lungs, and the combination of exposure and the chipping away at rock and stone seems finally to have caught up with Jude. He is agitated when he hears that Arabella is in town, and says that they ought to leave town. Mrs. Edlin, "the only friend we have in the world," has been helping to take care of him, and Jude doesn't wish to burden her any more. Jude really wants to return to Christminster, even though they may still be remembered there in somewhat scandalous circumstances. "I love the place-although I know how it hates all men like me," says Jude. Perhaps he wishes to go back to die there. It will be June in two or three weeks, and in June he has especial reason to be in Christminster. "Perhaps it will soon wake up and be generous. I pray so!" As Part Fifth ends, Jude and Sue are preparing to depart once again for Christminster, where the climactic action of the book is to occur.

Comment

Part Fifth is the ultimate calm before the storm. It is filled with foreboding: the symbol of disaster is the arrival of Little Father

Time, who as a human figure is unbelievable but as a symbol or wraith makes sense. He has been brought up through early childhood by the indifferent and selfish Arabella, without love, and he is therefore a classic study in what would today be called a deprived child, a potential delinquent and criminal. Hardy had none of the psychological terminology, but the basic idea that such a deprived childhood might result in violence was empirically known to him, as it was known to Shakespeare.

The shadow of death is on Jude as this part ends. What has kept him going was hope - the hope generated by his dream of Christminster. Love has not been what he has really found; the sensual attraction he has had for Arabella did not satisfy him, and indeed in some ways it had ruined him, though he conspired in his own ruin. But the spiritualized relationship with Sue has not fully satisfied Jude either. What has kept him going is the vision of Christminster - the pure vision of learning. And now he goes forth to put this vision to its ultimate test.

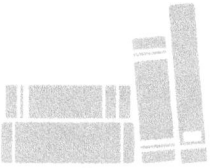

JUDE THE OBSCURE

TEXTUAL ANALYSIS

PART SIXTH

Part Sixth ("At Christminster Again"): Chapter One

As Jude, Sue, and their children arrive in Christminster again after such a long absence, it is in the midst of the celebration of Remembrance Day, a university festival. Jude considers it a "Humiliation Day" for him, rather than a festive occasion, because of his lost dreams and his lack of success in gaining entrance to the university. Jude is so eager to see the academic procession and the celebrations that the family neglects to find lodgings in town until after the procession.

Solemn and stately figures in blood-red robes begin to arrive at the colleges; meanwhile the sky is overcast, and thunder is heard. Little Father Time observes, "It do seem like the Judgment Day!" But it is only a procession. Jude interprets to the crowd outside the college buildings what the Latin inscription means on one of them, and further tells them about the masonry, some of which he himself had repaired a number of years earlier. As Jude talks-for his defect, if it is a defect, is that he tends to be carried away by his enthusiasm - a man, Jack Stagg, a former workmate of Jude's, recognizes him. Tinker Taylor, his old drinking-companion, is also there, and they talk. A general conversation, critical of Jude, grows among the crowd of lounging idlers. None of them has accomplished anything much except to stay alive during the intervening years, but they criticize Jude, saying that perhaps his powers weren't sufficient to gain him admission to the university. Sue begs him not to answer them; she knows how ill he has been and that it is not good for him to agitate himself over such things. "It was my poverty and not my will that consented to be beaten. It takes two or three generations to do what I tried to do in one; and my impulses-affections-vices perhaps they should be called-were too strong not to hamper a man without advantages; who should be as cold-blooded as a fish and as selfish as a pig to have a really good chance of being one of his country's worthies."

So Jude himself pronounces his own **epitaph** before the mocking crowd.

Jude is bitter now, and this consistent bitterness is a new aspect of his character. The crowd waits expectantly; a belated Doctor of the University arrives, the driver of whose cab gets out and begins savagely to kick his horse (again, cruelty to animals symbolizes in this book the cruelty of men to one another, and the cruelty of nature to man). Jude stands waiting for the learned doctors to parade out of the college; he is oblivious to the fact that it is raining, though Sue is worried about his catching cold, in view of his health. Sue has seen Richard Phillotson among the people on the other side of the street; she is grown cold with apprehension. But Jude says to her that she looks pale; she answers that Phillotson "is come up to Jerusalem to see the festival like the rest of us." This remark makes clear the symbolism of the last chapter. It is indeed a family which has journeyed up to Jerusalem, but the family is that of Jude and Sue. In fact, it is rather obvious that Hardy, in attempting to extract the last bit of meaning from his climactic section of the novel, is using the Christian symbolism of the trials of the Holy Family, and this is further reinforced when Jude and Sue are turned away from lodgings they have been at the point of renting. Sue and Jude finally locate a place, with separate rooms. The landlady asks her suddenly: "Are you really a married woman?" Sue goes into an explanation and as she is honest, she answers finally, "No." The landlady is embarrassed. The arrangement falls through, and Sue and Jude are asked to leave the next morning. As the chapter ends, Little Father Time says this to Sue: "I ought not to be born, ought I?"

Comment

We have detected a different tone as this part opens. Jude is much more bitter, and Sue is quite concerned about him, as well as apprehensive. The Christian symbolism will be subject to differing interpretations by each reader, but it certainly seems to be present. And the final, ultimate denial of life in the remark at the end of the chapter by Little Father Time is the herald of gloomy things to come.

Part Sixth: Chapter Two

This chapter chronicles one of the most famous occurrences in nineteenth-century English fiction. "Mother, what shall we do to-morrow?" asks Little Father Time. He knows that they must leave the following day, and thinks that Jude went away from the lodgings "to give us children room." The boy wishes that he hadn't been born. "I think that whenever children be born that are not wanted they should be killed directly, before their souls come to 'em ..." he says. At this point Sue tells him that there is to be another member in the family; that she is expecting another baby. Little Father Time is horrified. He reproaches her, and she tells him, herself quite upset, that he cannot understand but he will later. As he leaves and goes into the closet-like space adjoining the room, he says to her: "If we children was gone there'd be no trouble at all!" She tells him not to think that, and to go to sleep. But she doesn't take his state of deep, in fact pathological depression, seriously enough. After all, he is only a young boy, though this is a strange thought for him to voice.

The actual tragic **catastrophe**, as in the manner of Greek tragedy, take place, so to speak, off the stage. For the following morning, as Jude stands bending over a kettle to help prepare breakfast, he hears a shriek. It is Sue; she has fallen to the floor just within the door of the closet where the children have been sleeping. As he rushes to the door, he nearly collapses in horror: all of his children are dead, hanging from hooks at the back of the door which had been designed for hanging garments. Jude cuts the ropes from which they are hanging, but he cannot revive any of them; they are cold. Sue is in a fainting-fit. The doctor comes, but his presence is not necessary. The children had been hanging for over an hour.

A piece of paper is found in the chamber, in the handwriting of Little Father Time. It says:

"Done because we are too menny."

Upon seeing this, Sue goes into convulsions and is taken from the room to one on a lower floor. As Sue slightly recovers, she bitterly accuses herself as the responsible cause of the tragedy. But Jude comforts her. "It was his nature to do it. The doctor says there are such boys springing up amongst us ... the beginning of the coming universal wish not to live." This line, of course, is not any doctor's-it is Hardy himself speaking of what is happening in his age, as he sees it. But Jude's children are dead, by the suicidal hand of Little Father Time.

In a final, unbearable stroke of coincidental **irony**, the organ of the college chapel plays the anthem from the seventy-third Psalm: "Truly God is loving unto Israel." There is nothing to do for Sue and Jude but to await the coroner's inquest on these violent deaths. Sue accuses herself for not more directly explaining the facts of life to Little Father Time, who regarded her as in some way a betrayer when she told him that she was expecting another child. What she wanted to tell him, she tells Jude, is that it was not wholly in her power to give or to withhold life at a particular time - but she was too ashamed to say such things. The result had been the three deaths, and she continues to reproach herself for them and to become increasingly agitated.

"Things are as they are, and will be brought to their destined issue." So Jude says, quoting the chorus of Aeschylus' *Agamemnon*. This throws the occurrence of the triple deaths into the tragic perspective, as though Hardy fancies himself to be writing a Greek tragedy. At the funeral of the children, Sue has been kept away at first by Jude, but she goes there anyway, though in her condition she shouldn't have done so. She is wildly agitated, and Jude must take her home to the hated lodging-house where the tragedy occurred. The doctor is sent for, and there Sue gives birth prematurely to another child, but it, like all the others now, is dead. Sue and Jude are left only with each other.

Comment

The action of this chapter reaches such depths of pathos, if not formal tragedy, that it has struck some readers as excessive, disproportionate, even slightly on the ridiculous side. After all, Hardy uses coincidence perhaps more here than anywhere in this or any other novel: the coincidence of the playing of the hymn "Surely God is loving unto Israel," with the moment when Jude is cutting down the bodies of his children from the hooks. It is too much to be taken seriously, some have said.

Part Sixth: Chapter Three

Sue has recovered from this succession of grave shocks, though she has wished for death. She has regressed, and become as conservative in many ways as Jude had been when she first met him. For she regards the **catastrophe** as a judgment of God on them for their transgression of moral law. "We must conform!" So she tells Jude, who is amazed, and who tells her that the villain of the piece is "only man and senseless circumstance."

She and Jude discuss the final legalizing of their marriage, but decide against this. Sue begins to speak of the "solemnity" of their respective first marriages. It dawns of Jude that Sue still considers herself married to Phillotson, as the English Church does not recognize divorce. As Jude becomes a complete skeptic, and ceases to attend church, Sue has gone in the opposite direction, and now is strictly observant of all the forms of religion. "We should mortify the flesh - the terrible flesh - the curse of Adam!" So she says, and Jude does not quite know what to make of her complete change of heart.

Meanwhile, Jude is working again, at unexpectedly good wages. He is disturbed at Sue's reaction - her new piety and self-mortification - and he proposes again that they be married legally. But she refuses absolutely. She further says that she does not consider herself to be Jude's wife, and that they ought not to behave as man and wife, for she belongs to Richard Phillotson. Jude perceives that he and Sue have changed place intellectually.

Even as they debate the matter, Arabella suddenly appears. She has read of the tragedy in the newspapers, and has just come to them after visiting the graves of the children. She feels for the loss of her son, Little Father Time, and indeed seems more interested in him dead than alive. She quickly obtains one bit of information which she had wished to find from her visit to them: Sue and Jude are still not legally married. Arabella asks Jude for an explanation, but receives none. As Jude and Arabella talk further, Sue goes out. Arabella leaves for Alfredston, where she says she is staying with her father who has returned from Australia. Jude cannot find Sue, but he goes to St. Silas's Church. There, in the gloom, he finds her prostrate and sobbing. She couldn't bear it when Arabella came, because she believes that Arabella is indeed Jude's wife. "My babies have been taken from me to show me this! Arabella's child killing mine was a judgment - the right slaying the wrong." With this idea, she still says that she loves Jude as much as ever - only they cannot remain as they are. In terms of her religious views now, Sue is the wife of Phillotson, as she keeps insisting. Jude reminds her of what she had been, and the freedom of thought she had. But she says that these belonged to a different stage of her life; she has now seen the light and reformed, as a result of the harsh judgment of God upon her. Jude reproaches himself, as being the cause of Sue's misfortunes. After additional recriminations, they agree to live separately - "We'll be dear friends, just the same,

Jude, won't we?" Jude is again becoming the fated Christminster undergraduate in his relationship with Sue.

Comment

This chapter shows reversal and involution. Sue's motivation is more or less believable, as she is a creature of excess-either excessive liberality or, now, excessive self-torment and guilt feeling. Jude has become more hardened, and more nihilistic by the tragedy of the deaths of the children. He has long ago turned his back on his church. But he seems to think that Sue ought at least to be consistent, and this she is not.

The recriminations between Sue and Jude are not presented by Hardy in such a way as to make the reader sympathize greatly with either, though Jude seems more sinned against than sinning, when compared with both Arabella and Sue. His virtue, as Hardy presents it, lies chiefly in a native honesty and goodness of heart. But it has been abused, first by Arabella several times, and now even by Sue.

Part Sixth: Chapter Four

Richard Phillotson is still living at Marygreen; he is teaching in the little school there, and his old friend Gillingham still is the schoolmaster at Shaston. What is on Phillotson's mind is the information given him by Arabella to the effect that Sue was innocent of the crime of adultery which had furnished grounds for her divorce. Phillotson buys the weekly local newspaper, and in it reads a story: "Strange suicide of a stone-cutter's children." He finds himself upset at Sue's great misfortune, and he cannot understand how the age of the eldest child can be accurately given, for he did not know of the existence of Little Father Time or realize the Jude and Arabella had any children before their separation.

Arabella calls on Phillotson again, and tells him of the manner in which Jude and Sue are now living. She adds that they are not legally married, and never have been. And Sue is saying "that she's your wife in the eye of Heaven and the Church." Phillotson is amazed by all this news, and asks Arabella for the address of Sue and Jude. He plans to acquire Sue again as his wife. Due to the reverses he has suffered at the hands of society for letting Sue go to her lover, he has been somewhat broken down in terms of his moral idealism. Indeed, his main motivation seems to be that by re-marrying Sue "he might acquire some comfort, resume his old courses, perhaps return to the Shaston school, if not even to the church itself as a licentiate."

Phillotson therefore addresses a letter to Sue, offering to take her back. He is acting, he says, not out of passionate love but out of a wish to restore and salvage their lives. A few days later, Sue appears at Jude's lodgings; he is living again in Christminster. She will not come in, but she asks him to come with her to the cemetery. As they walk, she tells him that she is going to marry Phillotson again, though "only for form's sake ... because, I am his wife already. Nothing has changed that."

Then she suggests to Jude that he take back Arabella-exactly what Arabella has wanted. Sue is almost pathological on the whole subject of marriage, now, and speaks of herself as "a poor, wicked woman who is trying to mend!" Jude points out that she does not love Phillotson, and she admits this, but says that she will learn to love him by obeying him. Jude is moved to tears at this fantastic penance, as he sees it. But she is unshaken. As the chapter ends, they stand at the graves of their children. Sue tells

Jude that his worldly failure is to his credit - and this is another of Hardy's major points in this pessimistic work. "Remember that the best and greatest among mankind are those who do themselves no worldly good. Every successful man is more or less a selfish man." And the words with which she ends their relationship forever are: "Charity seeketh not her own."

Comment

This chapter illustrates Sue's impulsive movement from one extreme to the other. The explanation which Hardy gives or implies for Sue's conduct is really that of modern psychology- Sue has feelings of guilt over the death of the children, and seeks to be punished. Hardy himself does not attribute her actions to a genuine religious conversion. Meanwhile, the other two members of this foursome, Arabella and Phillotson: though in the eyes of society they are injured parties and are doing a noble action by taking back their erring spouses, actually they are proceeding from selfish motives. But the world will not make such fine moral distinctions.

Part Sixth: Chapter Five

Sue appears at Marygreen. When Phillotson meets her, she shrinks from embracing him-her instinct is still quite against marriage with him. But she forces herself to go through with the marriage. Sue recoils as she sees the marriage license. It represents final commitment. Mrs. Edlin, who is there for the ceremony, has left on Sue's bed a nightgown tastefully embroidered. But Sue seizes it and tears it to shreds, calling for something no better than sackcloth, for the other garment is "sinful." Mrs. Edlin, who is shrewd and observant, comments to her that she, Sue, is still in love with the other man, that is, Jude. She admits she is, but says that this is immaterial; she must marry Phillotson to pay for her sin. Meanwhile, Phillotson and Gillingham talk further. It appears that Phillotson will use "a little judicious severity" towards his wife, because his previous laxity had led to endless trouble. Indeed, there is more than a hint of sadism on his part, though it is unconscious. And Phillotson has right on his side, in the eyes of society; his only fault had been in not showing more strictness and severity toward Sue.

Comment

This chapter presents the subject of unconscious motivation in quite modern terms, although the language of Freudian and later psychology is, of course, absent. Hardy has apparently perceived, empirically, what happens in certain cases of sexual hysteria. It is true that Sue is outwardly doing the right thing. But her motivation is wrong: she is voluntarily re-marrying Phillotson, whom she does not love and never has, simply to punish herself. And neither religion, nor psychology, nor law, nor the state, has ever said that marriage is a punishment. Even in the religion to which Sue now subscribes, somewhat fanatically, marriage is considered of sacramental importance, if not actually a sacrament. And theologically, a sacrament can never be solely a punishment. Whereas her marriage is a self-administered punishment, and thus Hardy suggests that it is basically wrong, just as he further suggests that Phillotson's motives for contracting the marriage will not bear a searching examination. The marriage is wrong, then, on two grounds, but Hardy shows that society will think that it is right.

Part Sixth: Chapter Six

Arabella, who has been staying with her father, has been thrown out of the house by him. At the beginning of this chapter, she appears, looking rather shabby, on Jude's doorstep in Christminster. "I am lonely, destitute, and houseless." Jude is touched, and his good nature leads him to ask Arabella in, though rather against his will. He arranges a bed for her, and makes himself answerable for her conduct. Arabella seems meek and chastened. Actually, she has come, playing on his sympathy and what she knows to be his compassionate nature, because she wants him to marry her again. Arabella raises the question of Sue's remarriage. Jude asks her not to raise the subject; it is too painful for him to hear. But indirectly she persists. She finally offers to go to her friend Anny, at Alfredston, to hear more of the story and bring it back to Jude, and despite himself, Jude decides that he will assist her in this by paying for her travel. Jude has not heard anything from Sue since she left him at the cemetery, and he wants to know if they have married-Phillotson and Sue.

Arabella leaves. When she returns, it is with the news of the marriage. She tells him that she has heard the ceremony was "very sad and curious." And she adds the anecdote about the burning of Sue's embroidered nightgown. Jude cannot contain his emotion, and for the first time in many months, he goes to a public-house. Meanwhile Arabella has gone to visit her father, and tells him that she has the chance to marry again, but the scheme, for it is exactly that, will need his help. Her father will do anything to get rid of her, and tells her this to her face. But he will help her.

Arabella returns and finds Jude sitting in the public-house, mildly drunk. Arabella gets him going on liquor, and meanwhile speaks to him about Sue, while soothing and cajoling him. At the closing hour, he is unsteady, and Arabella prevails on him to come home to her father's house with her, as their landlord may turn them out if Jude appears drunk.

In liquor, Jude reproaches himself with his treatment of Sue. He was her seducer - "poor little girl!" As they enter the house, "the circumstances were not altogether unlike those of their entry into the cottage at Cresscombe, such a long time before." Arabella again is entrapping Jude.

Comment

In this chapter, the wheel is come full circle. Jude is apparently headed back to marry Arabella, and for much the same reason as Sue is marrying Phillotson, a feeling of guilt, though he doesn't realize this. He thinks that he must be punished because he has betrayed Sue. Subconsciously knowing that if he gets involved once again with Arabella, it will probably ruin him entirely, he goes ahead anyway. The truth seems to be that Jude no longer cares; he has been beaten down by life. So he half-consents to the plan of Arabella to take him into her custody, though he does not entirely know what he is doing.

Part Sixth: Chapter Seven

Arabella tells her father that she has Jude upstairs, and that the problem is to keep him around until she has once again become Mrs. Jude Fawley. Even her father thinks that this is a strange idea, but suddenly they both conclude that the idea is funny. All she asks of her father is that he be civil to Jude. She will do the rest. As Jude suffers from a hangover - and, added to this, he has not really recovered fully from his previous illness-Arabella works on him and he allows her to pay off the bill at his lodging-house and to have his belongings brought to her place. He is half-stupefied with illness, liquor, and above all his grief at the breakup with Sue, and allows Arabella to have her way. Arabella tells her father to have plenty of good liquor in the house for the next few days, and Arabella's father consents; the idea appeals to him, especially in his eagerness to marry off his daughter to anyone who will have her.

Mr. Donn has opened a little pork-and-sausage shop. Arabella tells him that if he were to have a party in Jude's honor, perhaps it would advertise the shop. He does this, and a number of idlers of the stamp of Tinker Taylor are invited. When the party is assembled in Mr. Donn's house, Arabella announces to the astonished guests that she and Jude are going to tie the knot again. Jude is indifferent to these words, scarcely hearing them. Meanwhile, Arabella has already made an arrangement with the clergyman in the vicinity. Then she launches the crucial part of her plot; then and there, she tells Jude that he has promised to marry her in the hearing of the guests at the party, not once, but several times. Jude hasn't said any such thing, but he has been drinking. Mr. Donn says that after all, marriage is the only honorable course Jude can take, because he has been living under his roof with Arabella for three or four days. "Don't say anything against my honor!" So Jude enjoins them. "I'd marry the W_____ of Babylon rather than do anything dishonorable!"

I will marry her, Jude tells himself and everybody else. And Jude, Arabella, and Mr. Donn as witness disappear then and there from the party to go to the church. Arabella already has the license. The guests gossip, until Jude and Arabella return. They are indeed married. As the chapter ends, Jude thinks of Sue's last words to him: "She said I ought to marry you again, and I have straightway. It is true religion! He-ha-ha.!"

JUDE THE OBSCURE

Comment

What has happened seems to have an absolute inevitability about it, as Hardy sets up the situation. Arabella will take what she can get, and through long experience she knows exactly how to work on Jude so that he will do what she asks. The trap is really a clumsy one. But knowing that Sue is finally married to Phillotson, Jude doesn't care what happens; he might just as well marry Arabella as not marry her. Here there is a further analysis on the part of Hardy of Jude's hidden wish to punish himself.

Part Sixth: Chapter Eight

It is three months after Jude's marriage to Arabella. He does done some work at his trade, but now his health is precarious. He is coughing as he sits before the fire. Arabella taxes him by saying that the marriage wasn't much of a bargain for her, because she will now have to support Jude. "Why didn't you keep your health, deceiving one like this?" Jude sees the ironic nature of the joke, and laughs at her: she had married him for a variety of selfish motives, and now she herself has lost out for a change. Jude gets worse. One day he asks Arabella if she will do something for him. It is to write to Sue. "I'm ill, and should like to see her-once again." Arabella is insulted, but though she tells Jude that he has no respect for marriage or its rights and duties (that, coming from Arabella and in view of her bigamy, her indifference to her child, and her complete selfishness, is hard to take!), she agrees to do as he asks, provided that she can remain in the room during their interview. He refuses, but she does not relent in her demand until Jude suddenly threatens extreme violence to her. "You couldn't kill the pig, but you could kill me!" But Arabella has once again lied. She wrote a letter, but she never posted it, and Jude after a few days suspects this to be the case. So he disappears-he has gone out, even in the foul weather. He is taking the train to Alfredston to see Sue. There he walks to the church, and finding a small boy, asks him to go to the schoolhouse and to ask Mrs. Phillotson if she will come to the church for a few minutes to see someone. She is aghast when she sees him, in his physical weakness, but she agrees to stay. She starts out by telling him that she has heard of his remarriage to Arabella, and that it is right of him to have done this. Jude is upset even more at this opinion of Sue, though he knows that it comes from her new attachment to her religion. He tells her that when they remarried, they had both been made drunk to do this: he on liquor, and she on a religious creed. She is tempted, but she regards what he is saying as sinful. Her lawful husband, though she admits that she doesn't love him and hasn't been living with him as man and wife, is Richard Phillotson. He suggests to her that they turn their back on all previous mistakes, and run away together. But Sue will not do this: "I've got over myself now." Jude has had a moment's happiness, in that he knows that Sue, insofar as she is capable of love, loves only him. As they part, each knowing that they will never see each other again in this life, Jude does not even turn his head to look at her. In a last instinct of human affection, Sue almost turns back to go to his help, as she knows how ill he is. But she controls herself. Jude goes back through the fields and to the railway station. The exposure is very likely to be fatal to him.

Comment

Jude has lost the will to live-again, in psychological terms he has a death-wish, all meaning for his life, as represented by Sue, having disappeared. But he does have one ultimate moment of happiness as he learns from Sue herself that she loves only him, though she will remain Phillotson's wife in name.

Part Sixth: Chapter Nine

Arabella is standing on the railway platform as Jude arrives from his visit to Sue. "You've done for yourself by this, young man," she says. Jude agrees, saying that it has been his intention to see Sue once more and to die; he has accomplished the one, and he doesn't care if the other happens now. As they walk home slowly, Jude tells her that he seems to see the spirits of the great ones of Christminster - the statesmen and scholars, from Wycliffe to Dr. Johnson to Gibbon to Walter Raleigh. But Arabella doesn't want to hear about them. "They bore me!" she says. And she reassures Jude that he won't die yet.

Meanwhile, at Marygreen, the Widow Edlin has come to the schoolmaster's house to help Sue Phillotson do some housework. Sue is a poor housekeeper, but she has been scrubbing the stairs "to discipline myself," as she tells Mrs. Edlin. They talk, and Sue tells the older woman that Jude has been to see her, and that she finds she still loves him, though of course this is sinful on her part. For penance, she has decided that she will give herself finally to her husband, Phillotson. Mrs. Eldin, who in her long life must have heard everything, is curious about Sue's motives and about the strange and incomplete marriage of Sue and Phillotson. But Sue cannot discuss this; she can say only, "No excuse is left me." She goes up to Phillotson, and confesses that she had let Jude kiss her. "Oh - the old story!" But she assures her husband that she will never see Jude again. Nevertheless, Phillotson, determined to treat her more firmly, brings out a New Testament, and asks her to swear this on it. Then she asks him to let her into his bedroom. She shrinks from him physically even while she offers this, but says that it is her duty. "A wild look of aversion passed over her face, but, clinching her teeth, she uttered no cry." As the chapter ends, it remains for Mrs. Edlin, as Greek chorus, to pronounce the words over the scene:

"Ah! Poor soul! Weddings be funerals, 'a b'lieve, nowadays, Fifty-five years ago, come fall, since my man and I married! Times have changed since then!"

Comment

The warfare between flesh and spirit is illustrated by Sue's final giving of herself to her husband. Whether it was morally right for her to have married Phillotson at all, in view of her instinctive physical revulsion from him, is a question not directly answered by Hardy. But the answer is implied all through the book, as part of Hardy's critique of the marriage customs of his day and what he saw as the hypocrisy which surrounded them. He makes it clear that Sue has remarried Phillotson only to punish herself, out of fanaticism, and that her motivation for ultimately giving herself to him is the same: punishment, not love or affection.

Part Sixth: Chapter Ten

Jude has, surprisingly, recovered somewhat, and until Christmas he works at his trade. But then his health breaks again. Arabella says that he has been clever, "to get a nurse for nothing by marrying me!" But he is perfectly indifferent to what she says. He says that he was never really strong enough physically to do the heavy work of a stone-cutter, but that he had felt that he could have done the work of a teacher and scholar, "to accumulate ideas and impart them to others." But due to the exclusiveness of the university, he had missed his life's work, and now, as a result of his having chosen a different kind of work, his life will soon end. Arabella regards his concern for books as simply a "craze." But she is incensed when he unconsciously calls her

"Sue" on one occasion. However, when she says that he is really quite ill, probably dying, she relents, and says that Jude may see her again. But he surprises her by saying that he doesn't wish to see her again. Sue has chosen her course.

Mrs. Edlin appears at the house of Arabella and Jude, and tells them, in answer to Jude's question, that Sue and Phillotson are no longer "only husband and wife in name." He asks when this began-it was the night that Jude had come to visit Sue for the last time. He knows well why she has done this: as punishment for herself. It is horrifying to him, and he speaks very bitterly of the lying **conventions** of his hypocritical society, which only succeeds in bringing on another fit of coughing. The doctor arrives, and he turns out to be Physician Vilbert. Jude, who has of course known him for years, expresses his opinion of Vilbert to his face very vehemently, so that the quack doctor runs back down the stairs. Even as her husband lies very close to death upstairs, Arabella offers Vilbert a drink downstairs, and in it she has poured, as she tells him later, a drop of the love-philter which she had bought from him at the agricultural show. "Clever woman! But you must be prepared for the consequences." And the doctor puts his arm around Arabella and kisses her. As he leaves, Arabella tells herself coldly, "Well, weak women must provide for a rainy day."

Comment

Here we see Jude's further weakening, at least physically. But his ideas haven't changed; indeed, they are more positive and intense. Hardy presents him as one who has been robbed by life, and who cries out in protest at what he considers the system which has robbed him.

Part Sixth: Chapter Eleven

Jude's life has dragged on until June, and Hardy's dramatic purpose in having this come about is clear. Again, it is coming near Remembrance Day, and the anniversary of the celebration at Christminster and the suicide of Jude's children. The weather is calm and clear. In the distance, the college bells ring. An evening party is being prepared in one of the colleges, and numbers of undergraduates with gay female companions drive up to the college doors.

The concert in the college awakens Jude. "The Remembrance games!" He calls for water, but Arabella has gone out and he is left alone. Jude begins reciting to himself verses of the Bible: "Let the day perish wherein I was born ... ." This, of course, is the beginning of the Book of Job. Meanwhile, Arabella has been walking around near the colleges. But idly she decides that she ought to be getting home. At her door she is met by several stone-workers, who have come to ask after her husband. "He's sleeping nicely, thank you," Arabella says to them.

But when she goes upstairs, she finds that Jude has expired, apparently peacefully. "She listened at his chest. All was still within. The bumping of near thirty years had ceased." Arabella asks herself, "Why did he die just now?" She seems unmoved; in fact her thought is almost that Jude seems to have died at that particular time just to spite her. Not telling the workmen of Jude's death, she goes off with them to see the boat-race and other festivities. It can't hurt her husband, her being away, now, she says.

She meets Physician Vilbert in the crowd. Arabella is suddenly worried. Under the law, if Jude is discovered to have died alone, an inquest might be necessary, and this would lead to some public questions about her conduct in leaving him to go out to a celebration. So she excuses herself from the doctor and the others and returns home. She seeks the assistance of another woman, and they lay Jude out for burial. That night, as he reposes on the bedstead in his lodging, covered with a sheet, there is the joyous throb at a waltz heard from the ballroom at one of the colleges.

Mrs. Edlin and Arabella, two days later, stand beside Jude's open coffin in the same room. Again there is the sound of cheering and revelry from outside. It is Remembrance Day again. Honorary degrees are being awarded by the university to the Duke of Hamptonshire and other illustrious men, and that explains the cheering.

Will Sue come? No. Jude had asked that she not be sent for. And she had sworn not to see him again, Mrs. Edlin tells Arabella. But whatever she may swear, and however much she may insist to her husband and others that she has found peace, it is clear that Sue loved only Jude, and will find peace only when she is "as he is now."

Comment

In this concluding chapter, the device of coincidence is used once more for ironic effect by Hardy. Jude dies and is made ready for burial at the moment that Remembrance Week begins. It is indeed a remembrance for him, too; it is a remembrance, as is the novel, for all those who have gone unwept into unhonored graves; for all those who are not the victors in society, but, like *Jude the Obscure*, the victims.

JUDE THE OBSCURE

CHARACTER ANALYSES

Jude Fawley

The hero, and the central character of the novel. Jude is the book, in his involvement in the lives of all the other major and minor characters, and in the meaning of his tragedy-if it is tragedy. For Hardy seemed bent on creating, amid humble origins, a tragic but obscure here, not the lofty and magnanimous tragic hero of the Greeks. Jude is perhaps in Hardy's view the ordinary man of his society, the outsider, denied access to opportunities for self-development and social advancement by a rigid class system. Jude, indeed, could be said to be closer to a Marxist literary hero than is any other Hardy character-except that it is not so much economic determinism but a sort of cosmic determinism, or the Greek concept of Fate or Necessity, which finally wrecks both his plans and his life.

There is an obscure curse on the Fawley family, and we receive hints of the operation of this curse back through the generations of the Fawleys. Jude, personally, seems to have many admirable traits of character, but there is a fatal flaw or weakness, perhaps a tragic flaw, or hamartia in Greek tragic terms, which ruins him.

Perhaps he aspires too high; his motivation toward a career in scholarship and the Church is, whether he perceives it or not directly, essentially selfish in its thrust. He wants to escape from a small village, Marygreen, where the life is intellectually and spiritually dead. Very well, but there is the suggestion that he conceals his real reason for his wish to pursue learning at the university. He uses the terminology of religious piety, but what he really wants is a non-religious end. Gradually, his essential honesty asserts itself, after the harm has been done, and he abandons his purpose for one more outwardly profane. In short, Hardy is rather ambivalent in his presentation of Jude's character, but his fate is one that moves us, as Hardy certainly intended, for Jude is basically a sympathetic character, defeated by the hardness of life. Jude is himself not hard; he cannot stand to see anything suffer, whether a dumb animal, a pig or a rabbit, or a human-even his wife Arabella.

Jude dies at age thirty, and there is the suggestion that he has been crucified by society. But those character traits which contributed to his downfall were not due to a basic corruption in him; they were comparatively venial, though not innocent. He seems to have strong physical passions with regard to women. But after all, he is a normal young man, and rather innocent about this aspect of his own nature, until he has been trapped by Arabella Donn. Also, he is prone to drink alcohol to excess upon occasion, although he is not a drunkard or in any danger of becoming one. This is not exactly the gravest of sins, comparatively.

Jude proceeds from faith and conservatism to skepticism and rather radical views on social questions. Politics hardly enters into the novel at all; Jude is not a political hero, and would really not do as a revolutionary. He does not think "approved" thoughts, in terms of what his society expects as a norm. But he does not act, or organize others to act to shatter the social stratification and "remold it nearer to the heart's desire." Probably Hardy's presentation of Jude's character and fate is more remarkable than we give him credit for today, because he has presented him convincingly. Writers of his own age were primarily writing for a middle-class reading audience. Jude is not middle-class; he is a workman, and is rebuffed by the colleges at Christminster to which he applies in part for this very reason. But what can be done by society to correct this snobbery and social imbalance? Hardy does not even suggest anything positive; he is more concerned to present a state of affairs negatively. But whether he is satirizing the conditions of university admission, or whether he is calling into question the unsatisfactory nature of modern life itself, is unresolved. Ultimately he is doing both. Jude is a modern hero, alienated from society and rebelling against its conventions. As he dies, Hardy uses him to accuse society - the horror is that he is indeed "obscure."

Arabella Donn

Jude's first wife. Hardy describes her in animalistic terms, and he begins to characterize her in this manner from the first moment Jude, by accident, meets her while she is tending her father's pigs and preparing pork for the market. Arabella is sometimes described as the "pig-woman." But she is more believable as a character, and more self-aware, than is Sue. Arabella is a schemer, as evidenced by her entrapment of Jude into marriage. But her motivations are always relatively uncomplicated: she wants to marry Jude so that she can escape from her unsatisfactory life as a pig-keeper's daughter, and she is absolutely unscrupulous in the way she goes about trapping Jude. "All's fair in love and war!" - this is the principle by which she acts. She gets rid of Jude, deserts him, in fact with complete indifference, and contracts a second, bigamous marriage with as little remorse as a cat shows in killing a mouse. As the book ends, she shows that she hasn't changed a bit from the selfish and unfeeling person she was at the beginning, for, knowing how Jude had suffered, she still was brazen enough to leave her newly-deceased husband, Jude, dead in his bed, and go downtown in Christminster to see the festivities of Remembrance Week. She only bethinks herself to return through fear of an inquest by the coroner on Jude's death.

But she is not a total monster. Jude is imposed upon by her, but he does not hate her. For one thing, she offers him frankly and without equivocation what he desires, especially as a young man, and that is the sexual relationship which Sue shrinks from. For another, there is a certain good-humored insolence about her which appeals to Jude. She has a tendency to moralize hypocritically, as when she describes her unwanted and unloved son, Little Father Time, as being the child of a lawful marriage- as if she really cared what was lawful and what was not. And she has an eye to the main chance, even becoming friendly with Physician Vilbert at the end, when she coldly realizes that Jude is going to die, so that she may have a protector and a means of support.

Sue Bridehead

An ethereal creature who denies the physical, described in the novel as "a female Shelley" because of her affinity to the Platonic orientation of the poet Shelley. She can give Jude everything he desires except that which Arabella offers him: the unabashed sexuality of an animal. She is, among other things, a classic case of sexual hysteria, which she is not able to admit to herself. Probably, as Jude himself realizes, she is unfit for normal marriage and therefore shouldn't have married Phillotson or anyone else.

She is more a vehicle for an idea - basically, the ideas on marriage of John Stuart Mill and other questioning Victorians - than a person, and some of her behavior, as witness the famous leap out the bedroom window, is pathological. At the end, she has become a fanatic; the sexual hysteria channeled into a rigid self-punishment. In her person, Hardy pleads for more honest self-knowledge by both men and women. But, in addition, he makes Sue a symbol of what marriage is. In short, Hardy may have intended to make Sue the embodiment of an idea, but despite himself he produced a subtle, rather clinical case study. Least of all did he create a living character in her. In her shrinking from the physical, and her wish to escape from it at any cost, she contrasts with Arabella, who uses the physical for whatever satisfaction and material comfort it will bring her.

Richard Phillotson

The schoolmaster who first, at Marygreen when Jude is a small boy, fires Jude with ambition to win a place in the university. Phillotson himself would be perhaps twenty years or more older than Jude, and when he appears after the initial scenes in Marygreen it is as a middle-aged, rather resigned man who acts even older than he looks. We never get a really good physical picture of him, or indeed of any character in the novel except Arabella, because of the tendency for Hardy to create two-dimensional characters who are symbols of ideas in this novel, perhaps more than in any other work of his. Phillotson, at any rate, suffers for his attempt to do the right thing by Sue when she wishes to leave him, and his character, too, is stunted, so that at the end there is a hint of sadism in his relation to his wife. He gives the impression of dryness, lack of vitality, deficiency in emotion, and a certain rawness of personality which makes him one whom no woman can stand. Yet he would be described as an upright and honorable person, who, in the terms of his society, falls from grace once, when he gives Sue her freedom to go to Jude. And this is the most uncharacteristic action of his life.

Little Father Time

A morose little boy, fantastically named since he was not christened in church. He is the son of Arabella by Jude, or so Arabella claims. He is completely a symbol, "of the coming universal wish not to live." As a symbol, but not a human being, he is one of the most unpleasant children in modern literature-Hardy, in his eagerness to make the boy exemplify of philosophical principle of nihilism or pessimism, makes him unbelievable as a character, and was criticized for this on artistic as well as moral grounds. He is so self-destructive, so skeptical of any good in life, that he kills the two younger children of Jude and then commits suicide, but the grand catastrophe is so excessive, and his character so unbelievable, that we have perhaps less sympathy for him than Hardy intended.

Farmer Troutham

A stout farmer at Marygreen who employs Jude as a young boy to keep his field clear of destructive birds, and who drives Jude off with blows when the boy shows himself so tender-hearted that he cannot pursue or frighten the birds.

Aunt Drusilla

Jude's great-aunt, and the relative with whom he lives in his boyhood, his parents both being dead. She is rather cantankerous, and lives to an advanced age. She helps to fulfill the function of a Greek chorus as well as a prophetess: she tells Jude of the sad marital history of the Fawleys, cursed by an obscure and unfriendly Fate. Basically, she is not without concern for the boy Jude, despite her gruff country manner, but the best advice she can give him is not to marry, and particularly to have nothing to do with his cousin, Sue, because marrying such a relative will only intensify the Fawley curse. But Jude does not heed this advice.

Physician Vilbert

A quack doctor, practicing in and about Marygreen for many years. A liar and a charlatan, who is not above tricking a young boy as he does Jude. He is of fantastic appearance, tall and bony. He contrives to trap Jude by conniving with Arabella, and at the end of the book it looks as though he will succeed Jude in possession of Arabella. His name is by its sound that of a "villain."

Gillingham

A friend of Phillotson, who gives him advice when Phillotson is thinking of giving his wife, Sue, her freedom to go off with her lover. A conservative yet rather sensible man, a schoolmaster about Phillotson's age, who also represents society in the mass.

Anny

A girlhood friend of Arabella, as coarse as she. She is aware of some of the tricks Arabella had pulled in order to entrap Jude, and one feels that Anny only wishes she had been as clever.

Mrs. Edlin

An elderly widow who has been a companion of Aunt Drusilla, and who is a friend and sympathizer of Jude and Sue. She, also, fulfills the function of a Greek Chorus, commenting to herself, with her traditional ways, on the folly of Sue's behavior.

The Christminster Undergraduate

A young man, never named, who became infatuated with Sue. He lived with her, virtuously sharing a sitting-room for over a year, and she denied him to the point where he became ill and died, leaving her a small legacy. Though he never appears in the book, he is a felt presence as he is Jude's predecessor in Sue's affections.

Mr. Cartlett

Arabella Donn's second husband, whom she originally marries bigamously, not telling him that she had been married before. A tavern-keeper, a rather coarse, red-faced man.

Uncle Joe and Tinker Taylor

Two of the drinking-companions whom Jude falls in with in Christminster. Tinkers, that is itinerant repairers of pots and pans, traditionally had a bad reputation in England.

JUDE THE OBSCURE

CRITICAL COMMENTARY

Hardy himself provided a definition of tragedy against which *Jude the Obscure* may be judged: "The best of tragedy-highest tragedy, in short, is that of the Worthy encompassed by the Inevitable. The tragedies of immoral and worthless people are not of the best." Tragedy, as Aristotle wrote, "is an imitation of an action that is serious, complete, and of a certain magnitude." Though Hardy must have had Aristotelian definitions of tragedy as well as the theory and practice of the great Greek dramatists in mind as he wrote the Wessex cycle of novels (he frequently refers to Aeschylus, and indeed Jude quotes Aeschylus' *Agamemnon* in Part Sixth, Chapter Two of the novel, over the bodies of his slaughtered children), it is primarily from the point of view of character that we must consider *Jude the Obscure* in terms of its attainment as classical tragedy. Was this Hardy's intention-to write a modern form of Greek tragedy? Put another way, can Jude be considered a tragic hero, or is he simply a pathetic victim of an inhuman, naturalistically ordered world where the iron laws of scientific determinism are operative? The answer to this question is a key to the evaluation of this work.

In the *Poetics*, Aristotle further spoke of the character of the tragic hero, which is to be elevated above the level of ordinary men. The tragic hero customarily suffers a reversal of fortune. And this reversal, or change of fortune, as Aristotle wrote in the famous Chapter XIII of the *Poetics*, "should not be from bad to good, but, reversely, from good to bad. It should come about as the result not of vice, but of some great error or frailty, in a character either such as we have described, or better rather than worse." But is Jude's downfall the result of vice, and does he attain to the level of tragic dignity? This has been a legitimate question to ask as we attempt to assess the greatness of the Wessex novels. For D. H. Lawrence, in his long and brilliant essay in *Phoenix* (see Bibliography), Jude, Tess, and other Hardy heroes do not fully reach the level of true tragedy. They do not struggle with gods or demigods, but, more meanly, with shallow social conventions. It would appear that Lawrence implied that Hardy, especially in Jude, was too much the social critic to be a tragedian; Lawrence's final word on the aspect of tragedy in the Wessex novels in general and Jude in particular is well worth noting, and indeed may be the best brief critical statement on this important matter: "There is a lack of sternness, there is a hesitating betwixt life and public opinion, which diminishes the Wessex novels from the rank of pure tragedy. It is not so much the eternal, immutable laws of being which are transgressed, it is not that vital life-forces are set in conflict with each other, bringing almost inevitable tragedy-yet not necessarily death, as we see in the most splendid Aeschylus. It is, in Wessex, that the individual succumbs to what is in its shallowest, public opinion, in its deepest, the human compact by which we live together, to form a community." Fortitude, strength, and opposition to cruel circumstances seem requisites of the tragic hero. And Jude has these, but he dies meanly rather than nobly, it may be. The question is an open one, but critics have generally been of the opinion of Lawrence that the achievement of the Wessex novels is not the purest tragedy.

A distinction should be made between the reception of *Jude the Obscure* upon its publication in 1895, and its critical reputation today. Students would do well to consult the reviews, signed and unsigned, appearing in newspapers such as the London Times and in literary and critical magazines, upon the publication of this novel. In general, it was believed that Hardy had gone too far in his questioning of Victorian social standards. In *Tess of the D'Urbervilles* (1891) Hardy had "faithfully presented" a "fallen woman," showing that Tess was essentially guiltless, that she had been sinned against that a woman in her circumstances may not have deserved the opprobrium visited by society upon those who transgressed a rigid moral code. Tess makes one mistake, her will only half-consenting. Ultimately she dies as a result of this mistake. But in Jude, the violation, the flouting of the conventional moral code is continuous; there is concubinage, bigamy, illegitimacy, entrapment into marriage, divorce-nor is the central character, Jude, really remorseful, even at his death, for what he has done. This led to a stormy reception indeed for the book; that it could have been published at all in England showed that by 1895 the peak of Victorianism had passed, and matters of sexual morality could be discussed with somewhat more freedom. But Hardy did not write another novel and, as has been pointed out, this was certainly due in part to his disappointment at the reception of *Jude*.

With his training as an architect, Hardy was extraordinarily aware of structure. In *Jude*, he attempted to follow the practice of Greek tragedy; there are rather fewer important characters in *Jude* than in most of Hardy's other novels. The plot of *Jude* is based on a symmetrical pattern of marriage, desertion, divorce, and final remarriage - thus Jude and Sue marry respectively Arabella and Phillotson, leave their mates and live with each other, obtain legal divorces, and though they are then free to marry neglect to do so. Ultimately they each remarry their former mates, though this step brings only further suffering and death. With this rather mechanical structure, Hardy is forced to make much more use of coincidence than was the case even in *Tess of the D'Urbervilles*, and many writers on this book have seen a serious weakness in the over-use of coincidence.

Hardy begins as a regionalist. He has an almost Wordsworthian affection for the lives of ordinary rural men and women who, in tune with their simple rural environments and in relative harmony with nature, can survive. Man, if he is simple and approaches nature with humility, may be happy. Such a traditionalist is the Widow Edlin; another is Jude's Aunt Drusilla. Characters such as these do not suffer excessively, in contrast to the more sophisticated and unsatisfied Jude and Sue, who both want something-success in the world of the universities and of London, romantic passion (though somewhat different in Sue's case), freedom from constraint, which is simply unavailable to them. This aspect of Hardy's work may be called "romantic primitivism."

But the regionalism of Jude and the other Wessex novels is a beginning, not a final end - and it has been modern criticism such as the work of Lord David Cecil, Albert Guerard, and D. H. Lawrence, which has discovered this. Hardy is accurate in his setting up a fictional region closely tied to an actual region, and describing it with a wealth of clear detail, so that the very towns and villages are identifiable. In this, the Wessex cycle represents the Yoknapatawpha cycle of novels of William Faulkner. But neither Hardy nor Faulkner is primarily a regionalist. Rather, Wessex, like Yoknapatawpha County, Mississippi, is a known area which comes to stand for an unknown-a dark region not in geography but in man's conscious personality and unconscious mind.

Thus Wessex, like Yoknapatawpha County, forms a stage for tragic action. The environment, the setting, the description of everyday life in unchanging rural England is important, but still secondary to the tragic interplay of character with environment. D. H. Lawrence, again in his essay on Hardy in Phoenix, could see the importance of deep psychological analysis especially in the case of Sue Bridehead, "one of the supremest products of our civilization ... and a product that well frightens us," as Lawrence wrote of her.

Our own age has gotten over the kind of response which Hardy's contemporaries made to *Jude*. Critics today do not see this novel as a success based on the scandalous. The enduring values of *Jude* go beyond regionalism and sensationalism. They do not lie primarily in the somewhat clumsy coincidental structure. Rather, *Jude's* ultimate worth for our own age seems to be in its unusual depth of psychological insight - and more, in its tragic vision. Whether it attains to the level of Aeschylus, Sophocles, and Euripides, or of Shakespeare, is a debatable point; most commentators would stop somewhat short of ranking Hardy with these on the scale ultimately literary value. Perhaps a tragedian is what may be called a cosmic critic, concerned more with the ultimate issues of good and evil than with local mores or social customs - and in *Jude the Obscure* there was a good deal of criticism of the merely transient social custom and prejudice. *Jude the Obscure*, then, may be evaluated as tragedy, even great tragedy, but tragedy marred by the intrusion of the local. Still, it is a moving work, and the fate of Jude can move us to pity and terror, though his fate is not that of Hamlet or of Oedipus.

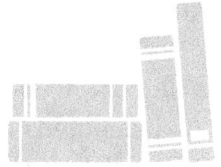

JUDE THE OBSCURE

ESSAY QUESTIONS AND ANSWERS

Question: What are the major aspects of his society which Hardy satirized in *Jude the Obscure*, and how effective was his satire?

Answer: It is perhaps superfluous to say that *Jude the Obscure* embodies a critical attitude toward the society in which its action takes place. Hardy especially singled out marriage, the Church and orthodox Christianity, and the English universities, for his social commentary and criticism. Jude is involved in all three, as aspirant, and ultimately as defeated victim. But Hardy was ambivalent towards his subject, for the impulse to satirize these specific areas comes into conflict with Hardy's wish to present Jude as a tragic figure, possessing innately that dignity which society would take from him.

As to marriage, whether legal or common-law: Jude becomes associated with two women who complement each other, but who are defective. He sees different things in Arabella and in Sue. What Hardy meant to satirize was outmoded laws and concepts of the marriage relationship. It was true, as has been pointed out earlier in many historical studies, that women had relatively few legal rights in marriage, even as late as Hardy's time. The husband was the master, and the wife was to bend to his will. Church and state together promoted this concept of marriage as domination, not as partnership. Sue fully subscribes to this view at the end of the novel, but her instinct at the deepest level makes her know that she is doing wrong, even as she swears on the Bible never to see Jude again. Divorce is not a solution to anything in the terms of this book; the clearest evidence of this is the remarriage of Jude to Arabella and of Sue to Phillotson. The essence of Sue's complaint against the institution of marriage is that it converts into a legal obligation that which should be so sacred and so entirely free, the mutual love of husband and wife. But the state she would substitute for marriage, whatever we may call it, does not seem to be any more attractive. And Hardy is not convincing as he shows Jude and Sue being persecuted by society, by gossip, loss of employment, etc., for their irregular union. Basically, they persecute themselves-especially through Sue's shrinking from the physical, which is an aspect of her character, not of the institution of marriage.

Hardy's criticism of the Church and of orthodox Christianity may be considered as his criticism of an institution which has become formalized and therefore, in his view, somewhat lacking in real life and in relevance to life. The symbol of the Church in *Jude the Obscure* is the theological library which Jude studies but finally burns, and also the stones of the churches which Jude repairs. But it will take more than the physical repair of the stones of the structures to rejuvenate the Church, in Hardy's view. It is perhaps a surprise to find, upon study of Hardy's biography, that he was a good churchman. But it is not a justifiable assumption that Hardy always spoke on this matter through Jude and Sue, for their opinions were at times contradictory. Sue runs the gamut from extreme free thought and skepticism to a rigid orthodoxy whose motivation is self-punishment on her part, while Jude begins as an aspirant for a career in the Church, and ends up at the position which Sue had originally held and which had shocked him. Hardy was questioning the relevance of the Church and its structure to his age, and especially did he call into question what he considered to be the destructive effects of its emphasis on forms, which amounted to fanaticism.

Finally, his criticism of the universities is related to what he implied about the Church, since the universities were the training grounds for careers in the Church and were originally Church foundations. Again, Hardy presents the spectacle of institutions grown old and solidified, to the point where they are denying to one like Jude the education and the intellectual liberation which he should have at least had the right to try for.

Question: What may be said to be particularly "modern" about this novel?

Answer: *Jude the Obscure* presents the classic posture of the twentieth-century literary hero in Western culture: that of the individual engaged in a war with society, and alienated from society. Jude and Sue, by virtue of their freedom of thought and their strange - because not fully motivated and explained - defiance of social conventions, are alienated.

The novel is thematically akin to many modern works which show young people - a young man like Jude - attempting to work out a code of ethics or an interpretation of reality to suit themselves, as they are not able in conscience to accept what society tells them. *Jude the Obscure* shows people trying to create or discover a set of values, having lost the ready-made ones presented to them by religion and by the state. Moreover, Hardy had shrewd, and often surprisingly advanced, psychological insights. He seems to have understood, rather beyond the understanding of many of his contemporaries in Victorian England, unconscious motivation. In Sue, he drew a picture of a case of sexual hysteria, though the term does not fully explain her, while in Arabella he drew a portrait of animal sexuality personified. He is obliged by the **conventions** of his age to hint at more than he reveals directly - the nature of the marriage of Sue and Phillotson, for example. But within these limits of **convention**, he attempted to treat his subject honestly, and did not write the books as a work of sensationalism.

Question: Contrast Arabella and Sue. What did Hardy mean to represent by these two markedly different women, both at some time such a strong influence on the life of Jude?

Answer: Sue and Arabella are complementary characters to the point where they each seem to be half, and that sometimes the worse half, of a single person. Their major contrast involves the physical. Arabella accepts her physical nature and uses it for everything she can get. Sue shrinks from the physical; she seems a Platonic Ideal. But neither approach is really one to promote the ultimate welfare of the individual concerned. Arabella does not see deeply into moral or philosophical questions, nor does she care at all for books or study-she thinks that Jude is wasting his time with these, and tells him so. Sue, on the other hand, is all intellect and speculation about how life should be lived. But Sue is at least as destructive to the men in her life as is Arabella, if not more so. The fact that she is less physical in her outlook than Arabella does not seem to make her morally superior. It is true that she appears to have far greater intelligence than Arabella, but due to her emotional and psychological peculiarities this intelligence is misused and ultimately brought under rigid and fanatical restraint. Arabella, a rather stupid woman though possessed of cunning, is unscrupulous and knows herself to be so; without a qualm she marries Cartlett in a bigamous union, she entraps Jude not once but twice-indeed more than twice - and each time relies on his good nature to help her. Hardy, then, seems to embody in these two women something of the same combat which he personified in Jude himself: "the deadly warfare between flesh and spirit." Further, Arabella stands for the world, the physical, in which Jude is enmeshed though not entirely against his will, while Sue stands for the ideal, though it is something which may be quite destructive. But she, too, is incomplete, and it may be that Hardy meant to signify by her that she - the pursuit of an ideal-managed to injure Jude more than the pursuit of Arabella did, because what Sue represented was really an imperfect ideal.

Question: Is *Jude the Obscure* a naturalistic novel?

Answer: The answer to this question is best given as a qualified "no." Literary naturalism, of course, is defined as the application of scientific determinism to fiction. The height of the naturalistic school or movement coincides with Hardy's lifetime, and from all evidence Hardy was acquainted with the writings of French, English, and American naturalists; it is interesting to remember that the greatest and most rigorous work of this movement in America, Theodore Dreiser's *An American Tragedy*, was published in 1925, three years before Hardy's death.

An American Tragedy presents its central character, a young man who resembles Jude in some ways and who goes to an early death in the electric chair as the convicted murderers of his sweetheart, as completely prey to heredity and environment, with no possibility of exerting free will to modify his situation. His life is determined for him; a combination of unfavorable family background, poverty, rather below-average intelligence, the hostility of society toward one who is assumed to be a seducer and a murderer-all these propel Clyde toward his doom. In the struggle of the strong and the weak in the social jungle - the survival of the fittest posited by Darwin-Clyde is among the weak, and the best that Dreiser can do is to show his compassion for the unfortunate and the obscure victims of the struggle.

But *Jude the Obscure* does not entirely follow the naturalistic formula of a passive, weak central character smashed by the hardness of life. Jude is as much a figure of Greek tragedy as he is a naturalistic hero; if one had to choose, it would be necessary to say that if anything he is closer to the former. He is superficially the ordinary member of society, but his ambitions and his potential, though underdeveloped, abilities are extraordinary. When he is weak, he knows that he is being weak, as in his relationship with Arabella. He has the final self-knowledge that the hero of Greek and Elizabethan tragedy attains to, but which is absent from the naturalistic hero, who is by and large genetically and environmentally incapable of attaining such knowledge of self. For the naturalists, man is a trapped animal, whose only hope is gradually to become aware of the harshness of his environment so that he can improve it by social and political action. But for Hardy, in all of his novels but especially in *Jude the Obscure*, there is an element of free-will and self-knowledge on the part of his important characters, however modified by environment, or fate, or coincidence. Therefore, *Jude the Obscure* is a tragic novel, but not primarily a work of naturalism.

Question: What is the function of the minor characters of *Jude the Obscure*?

Answer: In contrast to the four major characters, Jude, Arabella, Sue, and Phillotson, most of the other characters, especially Mrs.

Edlin, Gillingham, and Aunt Drusilla, serve as a sort of Greek Chorus-commenting, foretelling, moralizing. No character is casual and without a function in the book; Hardy is economical in his use of characters. Through the use of coincidence, Hardy shows the actions of even the most minor of the characters as they irrevocably affect the lives of the major characters.

Question: How effective is Hardy's characterization in *Jude the Obscure*?

Answer: This raises a serious question about Hardy's fictional technique in this novel. The social issues he develops for criticism seemed to be of such moment that Hardy may have failed, at least partially, to create absolutely alive characters. This is glaringly perceptible in the case of the fantastic boy, Little Father Time. He was probably never even intended by Hardy to be in any degree believable, for he is a symbol, an embodiment of a pessimistic idea. But Jude himself, as well as Sue, at times lacks reality-Sue of course more than Jude. Even in Sue's moments of greatest suffering we do not unreservedly sympathize with her, because it is too hard to believe in her. Jude himself is a pleasant young man, with some faults but no deep corruptions, and with many virtues. Sensuality in his downfall, and we can believe in this - but somehow at times he seems almost as unreal as his supposed son by Arabella, Little Father Time, who is totally unreal. Hardy fails in describing Jude's psychological, inward state, although this novel may properly seek psychological insight, and in other areas succeeds in doing so. If Hardy thought to make Jude and Sue great romantic rebels against society, he did not entirely succeed, because some of the ideas they embody, especially in the case of Sue, are manifestly self-contradictory and weaken whatever case Hardy seems to want to make: Sue shrinks from a normal marriage relationship with Phillotson, but she is almost equally as cold towards

Jude, and we learn that she had destroyed another man, her Christminster undergraduate with whom she had lived. Much has been made in Western literature of the theme of two against the world, of a couple giving up all for a great romantic passion. But as such star-crossed lovers, as a Romeo and Juliet, a Dante and Beatrice, even a Troilus and Criseyde, Jude and Sue do not measure up. And if Hardy intended them to be such romantic figures of single purpose, he failed in their characterization.

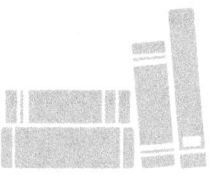

BIBLIOGRAPHY

Most of the essays and comments on *Jude the Obscure* are contained in general studies of Hardy. Of the books on Hardy's **themes** and literary techniques, the two listed under the name of Albert J. Guerard and the study by Lord David Cecil are especially useful. The work on Hardy by D. H. Lawrence includes, as might be expected, a long essay on the character of Sue Bridehead; it is a provocative analysis from the point of view of Hardy's treatment of the unconscious.

GENERAL: LIFE AND WORKS OF THOMAS HARDY

Blunden, Edmund, *Thomas Hardy*, New York: St. Martin's Press, 1941.

Brennecke, Ernest, Jr., *The Life of Thomas Hardy*, New York: Greenberg, Publisher, Inc., 1925.

Hardy, Florence Emily, *The Early Life of Thomas Hardy*, New York: The Macmillan Co., 1928.

Hardy, Florence Emily, *The Life of Thomas Hardy*, New York, 1933; reissued New York: St. Martin's Press, 1962.

Scott-James, R. A., *Thomas Hardy*, New York: London House, 1951.

Weber, Carl J., *Hardy of Wessex: His Life and Literary Career,* New York: Columbia University Press, 1940; 2nd ed. Hamden, Conn: Shoe String Press, 1962.

Wing, George, *Thomas Hardy,* New York: Grove (Evergreen Pilot, EP 22), 1963.

ESSAYS ON HARDY'S LIFE AND WORKS

Blunden, E. C., *Edmund Blunden,* New York: Horizon Press, 1961. "Notes on Visits to Thomas Hardy," pp. 272–78.

Ford, Ford Madox [Hueffer], *Portraits from Life,* Chapter VI, "Thomas Hardy," Boston: Houghton Mifflin, 1937, pp. 90–106.

Beatty, Jerome, Jr., ed. *The Saturday Review Gallery,* New York: Simon and Schuster, 1959. "Hardy at Max Gate," by H. M. Tomlinson, pp. 141–48.

BOOKS ON HARDY'S THEMES AND LITERARY TECHNIQUES

Beach, Joseph Warren, *The Technique of Thomas Hardy,* New York, 1922; reprinted New York: Russell Publ., 1961.

Cecil, Lord David, *Hardy the Novelist: An Essay in Criticism,* London: Constable, 1943.

Duffin, Henry C., *Thomas Hardy - A Study of the Wessex Novels, the Poems, and the Dynasts,* New York: Barnes and Noble, 1962.

Grimsditch, Herbert B., *Character and Environment in the Novels of Thomas Hardy,* New York: Russell Publ., 1962.

Guerard, Albert J., ed., *Hardy: A Collection of Critical Essays,* Englewood Cliffs, N.J.: Prentice-Hall, 1963.

Guerard, Albert J., *Thomas Hardy - The Novels and Stories,* Cambridge, Mass.: Harvard Univ. Press, 1949.

Rutland, William, *Thomas Hardy: A Study of His Writings and their Background,* New York: Russell Publ., 1962.

Webster, Harvey Curtis, *On a Darkling Plain,* Chicago: Univ. of Chicago Press, 1947.

ESSAYS ON HARDY'S THEMES AND TECHNIQUES

Howe, Irving, ed., *Modern Literary Criticism - An Anthology,* Boston: Beacon Press, 1958. "On a Criticism of Thomas Hardy," by Katherine Anne Porter, pp. 299–309.

Martin, Harold C., ed., *Style in Prose Fiction,* New York: Columbia Univ. Press, 1959. "Hardy and Burke's 'Sublime,'" by S. F. Johnson, pp. 55–86.

Lawrence, D. H., *"A Study of Thomas Hardy,"* in *Phoenix,* New York: Viking Press, 1936; reprinted 1961, pp. 398–516. [A brilliant and provocative discussion, especially applicable to *Jude the Obscure*]

Woolf, Virginia, *The Second Common Reader,* New York: Harcourt Brace, 1932. "The Novels of Thomas Hardy," pp. 266–80.

OTHER USEFUL WORKS

Holland, Clive, *Thomas Hardy's Wessex Scene,* Dorchester: Longman's (Dorchester) Ltd., 4, Cornhill, Dorchester, Doreet, England, 1948. [contains some useful illustrations and a local topographical index of Dorset]

Saxelby, F. Outwin, *A Thomas Hardy Dictionary: The Characters and Scenes of the Novels and Poems Alphabetically Arranged and Described.* London: G. Routledge, 1911. [contains maps; a useful work in finding the historical locations of the events in the Wessex novels]

It is recommended that students be aware of the need for study of the social and intellectual history of Hardy's age. Various introductory histories, especially those by George M. Trevelyan and Ramsay Muir, are particularly recommended.

SUGGESTED TOPICS FOR FURTHER RESEARCH, CRITICAL EXERCISES, AND TERM PAPERS

1. The place of *Jude the Obscure* in the Wessex cycle.

2. The storm over *Jude the Obscure* upon its publication.

3. *Jude the Obscure* as Greek tragedy; as naturalistic novel; as psychological novel.

4. Hardy's **satire** of

   a. Oxford University and English higher education in the latter part of the nineteenth century.
   b. marriage.
   c. the Church and orthodox Christianity.

5. A chronology and map of the action of *Jude the Obscure*.

6. Hardy's dramatic method.

7. Modernism, alienation, and abnormal psychology in *Jude the Obscure*.

8. Critical history of *Jude the Obscure* to the present.

9. Among *The Return of the Native*, *Jude the Obscure*, and *Tess of the d'Urbervilles*, which can be considered Hardy's greatest work, and why?

10. Hardy's methods of characterization.

11. Hardy's use of coincidence.

12. Concepts of determinism, Fate, and Necessity in Hardy's novels.

EXPLORE THE ENTIRE LIBRARY OF BRIGHT NOTES STUDY GUIDES

From Shakespeare to Sinclair Lewis and from Plato to Pearl S. Buck, The Bright Notes Study Guide library spans hundreds of volumes, providing clear and comprehensive insights into the world's greatest literature. Discover more, faster with the Bright Notes Study Guide to the classics you're reading today.

See the entire library of available
Bright Notes guides at **BrightNotes.com**

Available in print and digital wherever books are sold

INFLUENCE PUBLISHERS

www.ingramcontent.com/pod-product-compliance
Lightning Source LLC
LaVergne TN
LVHW021718060526
838200LV00050B/2724